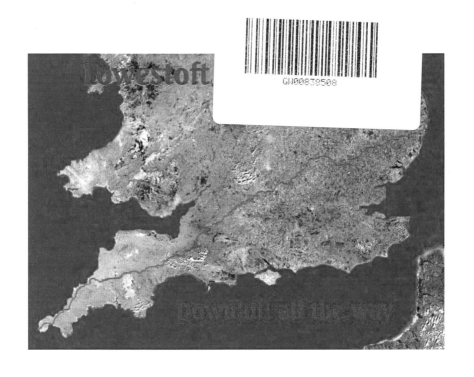

Cycling Across England

on

Back Roads and Byways.

For

Chris & Jan.

Hope you enjoy it

Phil Martin.

Phil

Downhill all the Way
by Phil Martin

Published by Aspect Design, February 2009

Designed and typeset by Phil Martin
and printed and bound by Aspect Design
89 Newtown Road, Malvern, Worcs. WR14 1AN
United Kingdom
Tel: 01684 561567
E-mail: books@aspect-design.net
www.aspect-design.net

ISBN 978-1-905795-28-4

Origins.

The idea of cycling across England first came to me in the early 1990s, when a gang of us were reasonably fit and used to do the annual London-Brighton Bike Ride. Looking at the map, the ironic motto "Downhill All the Way" sprang to mind immediately and is probably what kept the idea alive for fifteen years.

The simple reason for the choice of journey was that it goes from the eastern-most point in England to the most westerly. The direction was dictated by the relative flatness of East Anglia where one can work up the final modicum of fitness before tackling the hills of the West Country. Also, Lowestoft Ness doesn't make much of a destination after an epic ride, being hidden away behind the gas works, next to a fish processing plant.

My last two-week cycle tour had been exactly forty two years before I embarked on this ride, so it was time to set myself a challenge before advancing years caught up with me. With the demise of the much loved and respected Bartholomew's Half Inch maps, I found a substitute in a road atlas of slightly larger scale but much less detail.

Taking a huge gamble, I sat at our breakfast bar and began to trace a route across the maximum width of England along unclassified roads, lanes and B-roads. A-roads were used only as a last resort – a decision which the journey was to fully justify.

In order to keep the distance as short as possible - having chosen the greatest width! - I kept as close to the straight line between start and finish as the road network would allow. I did incorporate a loop northwards to avoid the web of main roads around Letchworth. It was no co-incidence that the same loop took my route very neatly around the top end of the Chiltern Hills and channelled me down the Vale of Aylesbury and the upper Thames Valley, between the Chilterns and the Cotswolds.

When in doubt or spoiled for choice, I resorted to Google-Earth on the computer and zoomed in from space on the lanes in question to take a look. I also researched accommodation on the Internet, with very limited success as it turned out. Tourist Information Centres proved to be a much more reliable source of help, but I only found this out the hard way.

Friday, August 31ˢᵗ 2007

Starting out.

With the weather forecast promising good things for the next few days, I kissed my wife Sue goodbye (my son Andy was still in bed), cycled down to Ledbury station and caught the 7.00 train to London. The bike had a reserved place; I didn't. My through ticket "Ledbury to Lowestoft" – and they can't sell *them* too often – included the London Underground journey from Paddington to Liverpool Street. However, when I reached the Underground station ticket barrier, having carried my heavily laden bike up and down stairs to get there, I was refused access to the platform.

Anticipating this scenario, I had researched alternatives and discovered that the famous black cab taxis can accommodate a mountain bike. So I laboriously retraced my steps across the station and went out to the taxi rank, where a notably reluctant cabbie eventually agreed to let the nasty, oily thing into his inner sanctum. It just squeezed in with less than an inch clearance.

A few minutes down the road, the driver thawed, turned on his intercom and asked me where I was going on the bike. My answer elicited the inevitable response "Why?" I suppose that from his seat it did seem a strange thing to do. However, the ice was broken and for the next twenty minutes our conversation ranged over travel, politics, immigrants, marriage and most of the other topics that he must discuss most days.

At Liverpool Street station I had time to buy a newspaper and a drink before boarding the Norwich train and stashing the bike securely in the allocated place. Leaving spot on time, it whisked me swiftly, smoothly and efficiently up the line to arrive, still on time, at Norwich. With only five minutes to spare, I scooted rapidly across the station to catch the local train to Lowestoft.

A further thirty five minutes later I alighted at Lowestoft station, or what passes for a station in Lowestoft. A platform, a bus shelter and some streetlights, with a sign on the frontage which proudly proclaims "British Rail. Lowestoft Central" as if the rail system was still nationalised and Lowestoft had several stations.

My bike, poised for action, on Lowestoft Central Station.

Before seeking out my starting point at Lowestoft Ness I found a souvenir shop and bought a Golly key ring mascot to join the Santiago de Compostela pilgrim's shell which already adorned my saddlebag.

Lowestoft Ness is behind the gas works, beside a fish processing plant.

Britain's eastern Cardinal Point is celebrated by the Euroscope, a 30' circle with a copper plaque at the centre and the compass points marked out in contrasting slabs.

Waiting until nobody was around, I did a quick change into my cycling gear. Then I waited until someone *was* around and asked them photograph me with one foot on the plaque.

It was time to put all the preparations behind me, place bum on saddle, feet on pedals and get going. At 2.18, with my handlebar computer set to zero miles, I did just that.

I threaded my way back through the town and followed the seafront road southwards. Inevitably, the roads on the ground bore no resemblance to the map and after passing Focus DIY, Halfords *et al*, I had to take a detour before picking up the planned route.

It didn't matter because pretty soon I was in the countryside. I couldn't tell you what Lowestoft smelled of - traffic fumes, presumably - but the first things I noticed were the quiet and the smell of new-mown grass. Taking a big lungful, I consciously let go and relaxed.

My unplanned deviation took me through Gisleham. I don't know how to pronounce it but there is a pretty church there, with an octagonal tower – a fairly common feature, it turned out.

On the way out of Gisleham, a brown rat erupted from the verge just in front of me, shot across the road and made a strange, four-footed leap to land belly-first in the long grass on the other side of the road. And then the clouds parted to give my first splash of sunshine since getting off the train.

After passing through Mutford, a pretty dormitory town, I re-joined the planned route. The lovely quiet lanes along which I pedalled augured well for the journey on which I was embarked, with good road surfaces, very little traffic and pleasant scenery on both sides.

As the miles passed, I began to regret my decision not to stop for food in Lowestoft, where there had been a very tempting chippie. But, just in time, Halesworth appeared ahead of me and instead of by-passing it as planned, I rode into town.

Halesworth town centre is pedestrianised and very picturesque, with lots of Georgian buildings. Among many nice looking pubs were the White Hart, White Lion and White Swan. The King Edward Restaurant served up a filling chicken sandwich, salad and crisps with a reviving pot of tea. Manna from Heaven.

Suitably rested and revived, I soon rattled off the remaining few miles to Huntingfield, where I had a room booked at the aptly named Huntingfield Inn.

The landlord and landlady, Steve and Sara Back, gave me a warm welcome and I was soon ensconced in my room. A flurry of texts to & fro with Sue and Andy was followed by a shower and a change of clothes. The shower was a nightmare. The pub's water supply is pumped from a well and this led to a battle of wits with the shower... which I lost!

I wandered down to the bar and gradually got talking to the locals – a good crowd who were keen to know about my little adventure. After a meal of home-made lasagne, chips and salad I staggered upstairs and was in bed and asleep before 10.00.

Day Mileage: 24.8   Total: 24.8

Archie, the pub's English mastiff.

The Longest day.

Up early, I perused the map of this part of Suffolk. The most notable feature was the number of disused airfields, showing what a godsend the flat countryside of East Anglia had been for the military planners in the run up to World War 2. And exactly where the airfields were needed: the part of England nearest to the enemy-to-be.

Outside the window masses of house martins swooped around, doubtless gathering in preparation for the long trek to winter quarters in Africa.

I accepted host Steve's offer of a full English breakfast and was swamped with food – the egg was even a double-yolker. Enough calories there to power a small army. This was the only time I went the whole hog as it took my digestive system forever to deal with it, but it had to be done once while I had the excuse.

Came time to settle the bill, and Steve and Sara not only filled my drink bottle with orange squash for me but donated £5 to the sponsorship fund.

Whilst I was loading the bike, Archie, their enormous English mastiff, came out, gave a token bark to fulfil his duties as guard dog and then came over for a fuss. As he warmed to my attentions, he gradually leaned on me until it took some effort to hold my ground. Once Steve had come out to see me off, seen my plight and rescued me, it was helmet on and here we go.

I had to backtrack to resume the official route so that after riding a mile, I was still quite close to the Huntingfield Inn, across the fields to my right.

In such flat country I regularly sighted church spires, both nearby and farther off, showing the whereabouts of settlements hidden in hollows or behind woods. However the need to keep my front wheel pointed towards Cornwall, had to override my natural instinct to go and explore, generating a slight frustration at what I was missing. But as it turned out, the day was to bring me a surfeit of pretty Suffolk villages.

Yoxford	5
Sibton	2¾
Peasenhall	2½

Stradbroke	7
Laxfield	2¾
Ubbeston	¾
B 1117	

Halesworth	6
Walpole	3
Huntingfield	1½
Heveningham	¼
B 1117	

Suffolk place names seemed exotic to a stranger passing through.

Approaching the four mile point, I passed a blue house with contrasting blue woodwork. It wasn't just blue – it was *BLUE !* With a blue garage and a blue garden shed to add to the blueness! I didn't stop to photograph them because I couldn't stand to ever look at them again! Of course, I regret that decision now because it would have made a great picture for this journal.

The first pretty village was Laxfield, which has the added bonuses for a touring cyclist of a small supermarket and a good pub, the George. It was too early in the day for me to need either. Laxfield has co-ordinated "yard sales" when households have stalls in their front gardens like a car boot sale without the cars. Carbon neutral, I suppose, and it must get the villagers socialising.

Leaving Laxfield I encountered a strong headwind which slowed my carefree progress and made me work harder for a living. After passing through Stradbroke the headwind was compensated by my first splash of sunlight, as the cloud cover began to break up. For this first part of the day I was able to crack on without the need to navigate as I was simply following the B1117, settling into a steady rhythm which let the miles fly by.

Approaching Eye, I became increasingly aware of what looked like castle ruins dominating the flat countryside from the top of a large motte. I went to investigate and, despite the protests of my long-suffering leg muscles, climbed the 92 steps to the top. I discovered that the "old castle ruins" were, in fact, mid 19th century.

The original castle had dated from soon after the Norman Conquest and was built by William Malet. After Hugh Bigod, Earl of Norfolk attacked the castle in 1173, during the rebellion against Henry II, it began to lose much of its strategic importance.

The castle was ruined by 1265 and was subsequently used as a prison. Later the mound became the site for a windmill, and finally had a folly built on it in 1844 by General Sir Edward Kerrison as a retirement gift to his batman. The folly collapsed in a storm in the 1960s and the remains are what we see today.

I'd love to know how the miller got the sacks of grain 50 feet up to that mill. Either he used donkeys, a winch driven by the windmill or a counterbalanced pulley system, whereby the descending sacks of flour hauled up the grain sacks.

Being the highest point in North Suffolk the castle mound makes a good spot from which to photograph the surrounding area, particularly Eye Church.

I rode on into Eye, where I discovered another historic small town centre. With pubs, shops, a post office and a couple of good cafés, it is a good staging post for the independent traveller.

Learning from the previous day, when I found myself getting very hungry mid-afternoon, I popped into the Co-op and bought two pork pies, two apples and some farmhouse oat flips. (No doubt the "farmhouse" is a factory but they turned out to be tasty and full of energy, looking and tasting rather like flapjacks).

I was surprised to see a lot of fields with cereal crops still standing and overdue for harvesting. Presumably the wet weather earlier in the summer had put all the combine harvesters behind schedule. A cheering sight in many of the fields was a second flush of wild poppies and daisies, bringing a warm glow to the view.

Either Suffolk drivers go faster than most or my stately progress gave me more time to notice things: I found myself totting up road-kill carcasses. By the end of the day I had seen around a dozen squirrels, four rabbits, several pheasants, a couple of pigeons, a stoat (or weasel), a duck and a red deer. Not only was I carbon-neutral but, to the best of my knowledge, I'd killed nothing at all.

Approaching Finningham I passed under a railway bridge over which I'd passed twenty five hours earlier, on the way to Norwich. My passage *under* was about 110 m.p.h. slower...

The railway bridge, shortly before my second crossing in 25 hours.

Garage sales or "yard sales" may be a Suffolk tradition – Finningham had seventeen garage sales going on (I didn't count them but a notice proudly proclaimed the fact). It is a good idea, saving a lot of hassle getting one's wares from, and back to, the house.

With no space for any wares, I cracked on, straight through the village, and continued clocking up the miles on my way to that far distant corner of the country.

As lunchtime came, I was approaching Wyverstone and found a good spot to sit and have lunch on the grass in the churchyard. My two pork pies added to my already heavy cholesterol count from the full English breakfast but they tasted wonderful. Maybe the accompanying apple and all the exercise saved me.

The church was delightful: simple and uncomplicated, it had a nice peaceful ambience inside. It was one of the few that I found unlocked – a sad reflection on the times in which we live.

As I got into the western side of Suffolk, the terrain became less gently undulating and more rolling hills. I paused at a stubble field, looking down on Thurston, to have a snack and text Sue. Like me, she had been enjoying sunshine, she told me, and had been sat in the garden but she was now indoors, driven there by grey clouds.

After diving down to the outskirts of Thurston, I was unable to find a little by-pass lane which I'd planned to take. Arriving on the edge of the town itselfA\\\\\\\Q, I had paused to consult the map when I was approached by a cheery little old lady with her trolley shopping basket. She asked if I needed help so I told her where I was going and we chatted for several minutes before I headed under the railway and turned west, out of town.

Along the road I found the other end of my proposed short-cut and was glad I'd failed to find the entrance to it – it was a gritty, overgrown, rough track. Perhaps the cheery old lady was my guardian angel...

Reaching Badwell Ash, I drank the last of the orange drink which Steve and Sara had given me and filled my drinking bottle with spring water which I bought from the local post office cum general store.

The shy, young country girl who was in sole charge appeared to be completely unperturbed by me, in lycra shorts and bright blue cycling vest, erupting into her shady, quiet little haven. It felt as if I may have been her first customer in several days.

Lunch – that waistline would reduce by the time I reached Journey's End!

The road to Land's End.

A mile out of Thurston I veered off southwards to skirt round Bury St Edmunds which, on satellite photographs, looks like a traffic nightmare for a cyclist. A pity, because it must surely be an interesting, historic town once you get to the old town centre. However, this little diversion from the straight and narrow paid handsome dividends because it took me through the village of Hawstead, where I passed the most spectacular front garden I've ever seen on a small house.

The village must have a thriving garden club - or else fiercely competitive neighbours – because there was a whole road full of beautiful gardens. Chris and Ken won my first prize (I deduced their names from their house name) for the sheer exuberance of their display. They should exhibit at Chelsea Flower Show.

The colourful front garden of "Chrisken".

A few miles down the road I passed through Hartest, which is picturesque in a completely different way. Hartest must have been beautiful for generations, if not centuries, because it's the village's layout and pretty old cottages that work the magic there. It would be interesting to see a picture from the 19th century.

Hartest village green.

By now it was twenty past four and I was starting to keep an eye open for overnight accommodation. There was nothing doing in Hartest, so I carried on to Stradishall which, near a major road junction, looked promising on the map. But no – I was through it in three minutes – not even a pub.

Down the road a few miles was Hundon. A lady talked about a house that used to do B&B but had changed hands... and she thought there might be a place over the hill and far away... I decided to crack on.

A couple more miles – and I was beginning to notice them by this stage – up the road I found a brown tourist road sign pointing to the Plough Inn, 1¾ miles away. I rattled off the mile and three quarters in a matter of minutes and there was the Plough Inn.

It was big; it was beautiful and through the bar window I could see a handpump bearing the badge of Woodforde's Wherry, one of my all time favourite beers. I love it when a plan comes together. I rang the doorbell – nothing. I rang again – nothing. The lights were on so I knew someone was in. I dug out my mobile and phoned their number, which was on the board outside the pub.

Eventually Sarah answered. I explained that I was a tired long-distance cyclist, in need of food, ale and a bed for the night. "I'm afraid we're fully booked?" I sagged. "Haverhill might be a good bet?" (Sarah was Australian). "There are some places there that do accommodation?"

Helmet on and back on the bike. Less keen now. Haverhill's name (pronounced Hayverhill) suggested some climbing to be done. My legs did not welcome this idea. It was slightly off route so, at Kedington – no B&B – I turned right to leave my route and go the shortest way to Haverhill. Sure enough I had a long slog uphill on the A143, very slowly, in a very low gear.

But then things improved with a long, 30 m.p.h. swoop down into the town. And, joy of joys, at the bottom of the hill the Red Cow pub which offered accommodation...   But not to me – once again, fully booked. By now the Sun was below the horizon and daylight was beginning to fade, as was I. The barmaid gave me very convoluted directions for the Woodlands Hotel.

It took about twenty minutes (or so it seemed) to find the hotel, only to get the same story "Got a wedding – fully booked". This was, after all, Saturday night. I explained my predicament, having checked and discovered that I'd cycled over 66 miles since breakfast. They suggested the Haverhill Travelodge, which was another couple of miles away.

Reluctant to waste more miles and time, I asked if they had the Travelodge phone number. The receptionist went off to find the number and was gone several minutes. When she re-appeared she said "I've had a brainwave – there's the room that the bridesmaids used to get themselves ready. We could clear that and set it up for you". I didn't tell her that a sack in a barn would have done just then; I simply said that would be fine.

While I waited, I ordered a pint and sat and watched the wedding party on the terrace and the younger kids making and chasing bubbles. I looked at the bike, thought about the sixty six miles and felt quite proud of myself. It occurred to me that while seeking accommodation I had passed lodgings for dogs, cats, horses and even – I kid you not – guinea pigs. But nothing for the honest cyclist a long way from home.

Once I'd secured the bike outside the room, I ran a bath, climbed in and luxuriated until I started to fall asleep. Then, dressed like a normal human being again, I went back to the bar to have another pint and a sandwich. I sat and chatted to the friendly staff for a while and then went back to the room, texted Sue to report progress and fell into bed.

Day mileage: 66.3 miles.   Total: 91 miles.

Sunday, September 2nd 2007.

Discovering Essex & Hertfordshire.

At the Woodlands Hotel, breakfast wasn't available until 9.00 so I had time to write up the diary and do preliminary packing before going down to my scrambled egg and bacon (no more full English – it takes too long to digest). Despite the early preparation, it was still 10.50 before I was on the road.

Incidentally, the accents in the hotel were pure Essex. The only genuine – and lovely – Suffolk accent I'd heard at all was a guy in Halesworth, where I'd stopped for my pot of tea the previous day.

It was a short pedal with a downhill start, to the edge of town – Haverhill stops at the by-pass and so does Suffolk. With the light industry of Haverhill on one side and, across the roundabout, a working farm the transit into Essex was quite dramatic.

Within half a mile I was surrounded by glorious farmland and the bustle of Haverhill was a fading memory, Civilisation still reared its head in the form of airliners on their way into Stansted Airport, but they weren't a big intrusion as they were more or less gliding, with engines idling quietly.

Descending into Steeple Bumpstead to rejoin my planned route, I was amused to note that the parish church doesn't actually have a steeple! Heading out on the other side of the village I realised how much I rely on my hearing when I passed someone using a hydraulic device of some sort behind a hedge. The rhythm just matched my wheel revolutions and, for several long seconds, the "Tsch Tsch Tsch" sounded exactly like the air escaping from a major puncture.

Subconsciously I'm always monitoring the bike for sounds of anything going awry. It constantly talks quietly to itself as we go along, so I just have to listen for changes or new noises. You're not aware that you're doing it until a change occurs, as I was to discover in Oxfordshire, but more of that later.

First warning of a car approaching from behind is the aerodynamic noise and unfortunately, particularly at speed, my back wheel makes a similar sound. I was forever clinging tight to the verge and wondering why they weren't coming past when there was no car there. I've since fitted a handlebar mirror.

The road to Land's End.

Essex's different style of architecture soon became apparent, with flint and brick topped with thatch much more common. I passed one cottage where the thatcher was actually on the roof, part way through the job. He, like me, was not welcoming the strengthening wind, which was blowing straight in my face.

I had tempted Fate by cycling towards the south-west because that's precisely where the prevailing wind comes from. But fate, in the form of an anti-cyclone west of Ireland, was smiling on me most of the time, for headwinds were to be a rarity throughout my journey and I wouldn't feel a drop of rain all the way.

A glimpse of my youth came down the road towards me in the shape of a Triumph TR2 classic sports car. I rode in one when I was a Boy Scout in the 1950s. I gave the thumbs-up to the driver, who responded with a wave and a happy grin. I guess he wouldn't have had many opportunities for open top motoring in the past few damp months.

I'd like to have been invited to this party...

In sharp contrast to Suffolk, Essex's harvest was all gathered in. I saw no standing crop at all.

At Radwinter I spotted the first church spire I'd seen since leaving Lowestoft. It was a small spire on a squat, solid tower but still a spire and the first one. And opposite the church – a sign of our times – the local sub-post office, newly closed down.

Unlike most of the roads and lanes I travelled – including those with grass down the middle – the B1053 was not much more than a cart track, with dreadful potholes and a badly broken up surface. It was like that until I reached Seward's End, just outside Saffron Walden, where they have re-built the road to a very high standard, with a mile or so of pristine tarmac. I suspect that a councillor or the local MP lives at Seward's End...

Saffron Walden was a huge disappointment. For a start, I encountered the first traffic lights and the heaviest traffic since Lowestoft. I had expected an idyllic, historic, old town but it's a terrible mish-mash of ancient and modern with no cohesion to anything. The church, where I had lunch in the sunshine, is very imposing, though somewhat sterile after the nice village churches I'd seen up to then.

The final insult was a lack of road signs which left me on the wrong road – up a long, steep hill to boot – out of town. My suspicions were confirmed by a lady cyclist going towards the town but I managed to navigate my way through a residential area to the right road, without having to go back down into town and climb out all over again.

Outside Starling's Green I crossed into Hertfordshire and as I was approaching Buntingford I was treated to the sight of my first buzzard of the tour, thermalling under greying skies. Then, after much guesswork, I settled on what I gauged must be the approximate line of the Greenwich Meridian. I took my own photo, using the self-timer, before spotting the official marker post in the undergrowth a few yards away. So I deleted that picture, cleared some of the undergrowth and took the one on the next page instead.

One foot in the east and one in the west.

Immediately beyond the Meridian, plastic wrapped flowers marked the site of a traffic accident. A car driver called Karl had overcooked it on a bend, lost control on the exit, gone off the road, hit a substantial iron post and a tree, somersaulted back onto the road and died somewhere during that process. It had happened so recently that the yellow markings of the police accident investigators were still visible on the road. Another young life wasted.

In Buntingford, I turned north to begin the long loop above all the busy towns and roads around Letchworth and Hitchin. This was the only, supposedly upward bump to spoil my dream of "Downhill All the Way". As previously mentioned, this loop would also – and not by chance – take me neatly round the end of the Chiltern Hills and down the valleys between them and the Cotswolds.

After the previous day's experience, I decided to phone ahead to a B&B that I'd found on the internet. Lovely website, shame about the greeting: "Not a chance!" and she hung up. Ah well, back to flog on and hope.

Approaching Sandon I startled a black squirrel, which shot off under a fence, banging its tail as it went. I'd never heard of black ones before but learned subsequently that they're quite common in that area. It was a pity it didn't stay around to have its photograph taken.

In Sandon I got chatting to a guy by the village pond. Like the lady yesterday, he knew a place "less than a mile up there" where they might do B&B. After very little consideration I decide to carry on – this was only 3.15 – and push my luck a bit further.

And another six miles of slogging against a rare, strong headwind brought me to Ashwell. This started to look like the same old story – a lovely old pub, The Three Tuns, offering accommodation. But this time, wonder of wonders, I was welcomed with open arms. The bike was quickly stashed in the lockup at the bottom of the back car park and I was soon ensconced in my room.

Arriving early, my first action was to wash socks, briefs and cycling vest. Only when they were hanging up to dry did I discover that my second cycling vest was not where it should be, in my saddlebag but still hanging in the wardrobe at home in Wellington Heath! I now had to hope that this one would dry by morning.

I'd just finished the washing when I found myself dashing to the window in response to a familiar sound – the Rolls Royce Merlin aero-engine. Quite low overhead roared a Spitfire and a Sea Fury, hotly pursued by a second Spitfire and a Hurricane. A very nostalgic sight and sound.

Two cups of tea, a shower and a change of clothes later I headed down to the bar to see what was on offer. I was soon enjoying a pint of – appropriately – Olde Trip Ale and awaiting the arrival of dinner. I had a second pint (not Olde Trip, which is a mite powerful) with some delicious lamb chops. I lingered for a while, nattering to some locals, and then headed for my bed.

Day mileage: 45.7   Total: 137

Monday, September 3rd 2007.

Over the Hills and Far Away.

A cold front going through in the night took away the strong winds and left a fresh, sunny morning. My cycling vest did dry overnight and after breakfast, with my long-sleeved jersey on top of the vest, I set off up the hill out of Ashwell.

As soon as I cleared trees and houses and looked ahead, I could see that the countryside was flatter than yesterday which, with the absence of the wind, was welcome news.

Hertfordshire was even more advanced with the harvest. Not only was it gathered in but the straw bales had been taken to store and the stubble fields were being rolled, harrowed or ploughed in.

As I entered Bedfordshire, I reached the top of the bulge in my route and began to head due west, crossing the busy A1 dual carriageway. The Chilterns were still safely out of the way to my left, where they would be for most of the next two days as I slid down the Vale of Aylesbury and then the Thames Valley.

I passed a huge, solidly built, concrete water tower with another one, six or eight miles to the south-west and a third a similar distance beyond that. They were built in 1934, presumably as part of the original provision of mains water to the area.

For several miles I was hemmed in by "commuterland", with small dormitory towns like Clifton and Shefford. Fussy, uniform, characterless collections of houses and small shops with nothing much happening because everybody had gone off to work.

My route committed me to an unavoidable mile and a half down the fast and busy A507. Joyfully, when I reached it, I found that Bedfordshire County Council had provided a good cycleway beside it. Even so, it was a relief to escape back to open countryside at Beadlow and glimpse Top Farm across the fields.

Top Farm, Note the flat countryside – good news for the touring cyclist.

A friendly local?

My next port of call was Clophill, a pretty village straddling the A6 trunk road. Suddenly the architecture was mainly red brick – a sure sign that I was approaching the Bedfordshire brickfields. I parked the bike on the village green, took off my helmet and sat on a wooden seat to look at the map and survey the scenery for twenty minutes.

A proper, old-fashioned (and thriving) village shop gave me the opportunity to top up my drink bottle and take on stores for lunchtime. The shop was quite a hub of the community, with villagers standing outside catching up on the news or just passing the time of day. A rare sight in these busy, bustling, modern times. Two pubs faced onto the green, The Green Man and the Flying Horse, but it was too early in the day to start tippling.

The Flying Horse was a Beefeater house but the Green Man, like the vast majority of the pubs I had passed so far, was owned by Greene King.

As they are an East Anglian outfit, I had expected to escape their clutches by this stage but had forgotten that they have taken over Morland's Brewery. Consequently their empire now spans half the country. Most Greene King pubs are well run and their ales, especially Abbot Ale, are fine but to a real ale enthusiast, variety is the breath of life and I was keen to try some local brews.

Beyond Clophill the contours began to undulate once again and a couple of miles along the road, at Maulden, I stopped at the slightly elevated parish church to look around. Inside the church someone was playing the organ, so I left them in peace and listened from outside as I took in the view. It was too hazy to make a decent photo but it was pleasant enough and a few miles off, I could see the third of my 1934 water towers.

Approaching Ampthill, it became abundantly clear how it acquired its name. I don't know what "Ampt" refers to but the second half of its name is very appropriate – all at once I was up and down like a roller-coaster.

In turning left to pass through the town centre, I resumed my south-westerly heading and entered the Vale of Aylesbury. I had completed my upward bulge and was back onto a straight(ish) line for Land's End.

Clophill village green and its two pubs.

Ampthill, built mainly of Bedfordshire red bricks.

It was late morning, after passing Steppingley and just before crossing the M1 motorway, when I felt warm enough to take off the long-sleeved jersey. The cooler air was a small price to pay for the sunshine brought by the previous night's cold front.

The M1 Motorway – a reminder of what I had escaped for a couple of weeks...

I couldn't have planned my lunch stop better if I'd tried – Woburn Deer Park. Sitting under an oak tree, shaded from the glorious sunshine, I watched several different groups of deer, fallow, red and muntjac, wandering across the grass, quite close to me and quite unconcerned.

...and, in contrast, Woburn Deer Park.

South of me I could see a glider from the London Gliding Club at Dunstable Downs, working the thermals of this pleasant day. Meanwhile in Ledbury, I discovered, Sue was enduring a cold, drizzly day – truly I was blessed.

All too soon it was time to collect various lunch wrappings, bottle and camera and get back on the bike. On the sloping road out of the deer park I exceeded the 30 mph speed limit, without hazarding the deer or other road users – there weren't any.

Like Ampthill, Little Brickhill lived up to its name – the "Little" plainly refers to the village and not the hill – and made me do some hard work before enjoying its charms. However, an excellent pint of Abbot Ale at the Old Green Man revived me no end. I was horrified to discover that I was drinking my pint in the unitary authority of Milton Keynes! It always used to be Buckinghamshire.

On the road between Little Brickhill and Great Brickhill, apart from entering Buckinghamshire, county of my birth, I passed several heaps of yellow sand at the roadside. Not the work of the local authority but badgers!

After Great Brickhill there followed a long, death-defying swoop down to the Grand Union Canal at Three Locks. I reached the dizzy speed of 34.9 mph – a suitable reward for all the hard work getting up to the Brickhills. Whilst plummeting down the hill I saw two vivid blue, 100 foot long streaks along the far side of the road. Each included a tin lid, showing that the streaks were the result of 2½ litre cans of paint falling – or being thrown – from a fast moving vehicle. Some people lead exciting lives...

Visiting Three Locks was an ambition achieved after more than forty years. I used to cycle past there (in a different direction) in the 1960s, on my way to and from training courses at the now famous Bletchley Park. Always too eager to get home or get to the college, I'd never taken the time to stop and explore.

It was as pretty as I'd always imagined it would be. I took some photos and then went to help a bright green canal boat through the top lock, as the helmsman was alone on board. We got talking and when he found out what I was doing, he donated £5 to my funds, bless him. His boat was named after the blues singer Muddy Waters – a nice play on words.

Three Locks, with the Muddy Waters exiting the middle lock.

I took a breather at Dunton and photographed the pretty little church there. Later, and several miles down the road, I realised that I'd put my helmet on back to front! Having subsequently re-created the effect in front of a mirror, I'm very glad I didn't meet anybody whom I needed to impress... (Sorry, no photo available!)

Dunton Church.

The afternoon was slipping by and I was getting into my familiar situation of searching for overnight accommodation. I phoned ahead to the Lion at Waddesdon but there was no reply. Nothing for it but to plough on and keep my eyes open. I passed two lovely pubs in Whitchurch but neither offered B&B. So... plough on. Then, a couple of miles from Waddesdon, a second phone call brought reassuring news – the Lion had one room free and they couldn't have been more welcoming. When I got there, they found a home for the bike and were very hospitable.

I had a phone call from Sue to say that her car had a suspected blown cylinder head gasket – it picked its moment. A second phone call from an old friend, Esther Lewis, suggested meeting her and husband Dave for a pub lunch the following day. We agreed to meet at the Barley Mow at Clifton Hamden.

The Lion did me proud, with good food and excellent ale (a foretaste of Cornwall with a pint of St Austell Brewery's Tribute Ale). My room was good and the only slight fly in the ointment was the heavy traffic on the A40, just outside the window but I soon adjusted to that and went out like a light.

Day mileage: 46.3   Total: 184

Tuesday, September 4th 2007.

In My Father's Wheel Tracks.

With around twenty five miles to ride before lunch at Clifton Hampden, I needed to be on the road in good time, so breakfast was at 7.00 o'clock. Waddesdon was a mile off my route, on a hill, so I had a nice start to the day, freewheeling down the pavement with the rush-hour commuter traffic roaring past on the A40.

At the bottom of the hill I seized my moment and dashed across the main road, through the mayhem, to escape down the minor road which was the resumption of my route to Land's End.

It was chilly in the valley, with just a hint of mist, and I could actually see the brown pollution haze building up over Aylesbury as the cars poured into the town. I was just getting into a rhythm when I hit a long, steep, unrelenting hill. It was a bit of a sharp wake-up call after my easy start, and I was soon glad of the quick massage I'd given my thigh muscles at the Lion before setting out.

At the top of the hill, I was clear of the mist and could see the Chilterns over to my left with Stokenchurch telecommunications tower (not visible in the photograph which follows) looming over the back of the ridge. In the 1980s I flew a glider there from Swindon, flew round it and photographed it for my 50 kilometre flight.

It occurred to me that I was getting into my late Dad's old haunts. Living near Slough for over forty years and never owning a car, he cycled around this neck of the woods a lot. When he died, aged 81, I did some research and know for certain that in his lifetime he cycled well over one hundred thousand miles.

Chearsley was a pretty, sleepy, little village but, once again, my schedule left no time for lingering to explore. In the distance I could see Didcot Power Station cooling towers generating their own, small cloud – a useful reference point as they are only a few miles from Clifton Hampden.

In the distance is Didcot Power Station, generating its own cloud.

36

Approaching the outskirts of Thame, I left Buckinghamshire and entered Oxfordshire. I was amused to see the name of the Thame Travelodge hotel: situated on a hectic, fiendishly busy roundabout, it is called "Sleepy Hollow".

Thame was a revelation and little changed since I was last there, say thirty years ago, or even when I used to cycle there from Slough forty five years ago. It is a thriving, bustling market town which has managed to retain all of its traditional character, yet doesn't feel old fashioned and has a happy feel to it.

Thame.

Not far out of Thame, the road passed smack through the middle of a large rookery. There were dozens of them, on both sides of the road, all shouting the odds and there was no way of knowing what they were saying.

Approaching the M40, a buzzard called from overhead, as they do on good thermalling days. I was well ahead of schedule and so decided to text Esther and Dave to suggest meeting them further along the road. While awaiting their reply I had a look at the route ahead on the map. What I didn't do was re-fasten the bottom of the map holder. Suddenly I became aware of half my map sheets lying on the road, being stirred up by the breeze!

I quickly chased around, retrieved them and was sorting them into numerical order when a car came round the corner and ran over one that I'd missed. So I now had one map sheet embossed with an impression of Oxfordshire highway. I may sell it to the Tate Modern – I'm sure I could think up some pretentious blurb...

No reply to my text to Esther, so I cracked on, entering a 15 mile section of the route where I had to twist and turn a fair bit to fiddle my way round various industrial areas and cross the River Thames.

After crossing the M40, a beautiful Red Kite glided serenely by, low over my head. There are lots of them around there because the Chilterns were one of the RSPB's first release areas for captive bred Red Kites. With the kite still in sight, I stopped to shed my jersey and almost trod on a young rabbit hiding in the grass at the side of the road. I didn't tell the kite.

Another reminder of gliding days – I passed a road sign to Pyrton, where I landed after my flight round Stokenchurch Tower. As I was making the glider safe, a sweet lady with a straw hat and a butterfly net came over and asked if the wind had stopped. (In fact I'd run out of thermals: something completely different).

On the approach to Chalgrove, my subconscious auditory monitoring system alerted me to a developing rattle from the back of the bike. It was a screw on the bracket holding the back mudguard. I trolleyed on and found a safe, quiet spot to work on the bike.

Because of the design of the bike – bless those designers – I would have to remove the wheel *and* the mudguard in order to reach the screw. To do this, I would have to turn the bike upside down. To do *that,* I would have to remove the saddlebag *and* the handlebar bag *and* the drink bottle. BLESS those designers!

I removed the handlebar bag first, because its weight gives the front wheel a mind of its own. Then the saddlebag and bottle, standing them all carefully on the ground. I turned the bike upside down and removed the wheel (bear in mind that this is the back wheel, with the 7-speed gears to contend with).

As I was putting the wheel to one side, the bike toppled over. In doing so, it contrived to drape the chain across my saddlebag in such a way that the chain unwrapped the polythene cover on my nice, new, bright yellow waterproof jacket and smeared dirty chain oil right across the jacket! Scientists and engineers would have to work for *years* to design something that would do that reliably.

I was not best pleased, as anybody within a hundred yards would have known... This was obviously my day for being outwitted by inanimate objects. The actual repair took about two minutes. Cleaning the waterproof, when I got home, took an hour.

The scene of the mini-drama.

With everything back together and composure regained, I carried on up the road to the monument to John Hampden at the site of the Battle of Chalgrove Field (English Civil War). I educated myself about this small piece of English history with the help of the excellent, informative notice beside the monument.

The battle, which in fact was little more than a skirmish, was won by the Royalists, thanks to the quick wittedness of their commander, Prince Rupert.

The inscription on the monument reads:

Here in the field of Chalgrove,
John Hampden, after an able and strenuous but
unsuccessful resistance, in Parliament and before
the judges of the land,
to the measures of an arbitrary court,
first took arms, assembling the levies of the
associated counties of Buckingham and Oxford in
1642.

Within a few paces of this spot he received the
wound from which he died
while fighting in defence of the free monarchy
and liberties of England.
June 18th 1643

In the 200th year from that day this stone was
raised in reverence to his memory.
June 18th 1843

Nearby is a memorial to the USAF air-crew who were based at Chalgrove Airfield, dedicated exactly 150 years after the monument.

CHALGROVE AIRFIELD
STATION 465

TO THE MEMORY OF AMERICAN SERVICEMEN WHO WERE BASED HERE DURING WORLD WAR TWO. THEY SERVED WITH THE 10TH PHOTOGRAPHIC RECONNAISSANCE GROUP AND TROOP CARRIER PATHFINDER GROUP (PROV.) OF THE 9TH UNITED STATES ARMY AIR FORCE, AIRBORNE PATHFINDER PARATROOPS OF THE U.S. ARMY AND THE 7TH PHOTOGRAPHIC RECONNAISSANCE GROUP, THE "EYES OF THE 8TH"UNITED STATES ARMY AIR FORCE.
MAY THEY NEVER BE FORGOTTEN
DEDICATED JUNE 18TH 1993

One end of the airfield is now home to Martin Baker Ejector Seats. While I was at the memorial a siren sounded and after a few seconds there was a whoosh, lasting a second or so. They must have been testing an ejector seat. Back on the bike and further along the road I was able to see the testing rig behind the factory.

As I went past the south side of the airfield I saw the now abandoned old road, off to my left, along which I cycled the last time I was at Chalgrove, on a chilly morning 47 or 48 years ago.

Stadhampton, another pretty village, was home to a pub called the Crown and it's owned by – guess who – Greene King. The Coach and Horses at Chiselhampton, on the other hand, is a free house. I know which one I would have visited, had I not had a prior engagement.

I reached Clifton Hampden at 12.10 with no answering text from Esther and Dave, so I phoned them from outside the Barley Mow. They had their mobile on silent and simply hadn't seen my texts. They were about half an hour away so I sat in the sunshine and tweaked the bike while I waited for them to arrive.

When they did arrive, it wasn't just Esther and Dave but their kids, Nicholas and Rachel, and Dave's dad Charles, as well. We trooped into the Barley Mow, only to be greeted by a blackboard proclaiming that all five real ales were off because of "a gas pipe problem".

The words gas and real ale should never, ever occur in the same sentence, so we made mental notes about the Barley Mow's idea of real ale and decamped to the George Inn, back over the river. By a strange co-incidence they were serving St Austell Brewery's Tribute Ale, which I had imbibed at the Lion, the previous evening.

We settled in the sunlit pub garden and were trying to make sense of the menu when, all at once and out of nowhere, there was Esther's sister Helen, with her little toddler Heather, aged 2 – there had been a conspiracy. It was good to be surrounded by friends for a while.

After a lot of confusion with the menu, which incorporated some quirky, trendy nonsense which the Polish waitress couldn't explain properly, we settled down to lunch in the garden. When the food arrived, it was really good. They would have done so much better to have presented it through a simple menu.

After lunch we all got together for a group photo before going our separate ways.

In their cars they obviously left me for dead, so I pottered over the Thames for the third time, cast a withering glance at the Barley Mow, and paused a little farther along the river bank to take a photo.

Thames-side Tranquillity.

Trolleying contentedly down the road, having been treated to two pints of good ale and my lunch by my good friends, I entered Long Wittenham. Rounding a corner into the village, I found all seven of them lined along the side of the road with flags and hooters, waving me through like the winner of the Tour de France!

Some miles later, between Drayton and Steventon, the Lewises caught up with me again and came past to the sound of much tooting of the car horn and with Dave taking my photo from the car window.

Reaching Steventon, I phoned ahead to the B&B for which I was aiming, where they were supposed to welcome cyclists, only to find that it had closed down over a year earlier. So much for the internet.

With no other firm contacts and having clocked up enough miles for the day, I decide to play safe. I called in to the Fox pub, but they had building work going on and reduced accommodation, so no vacancies. The landlady told me about a couple of B&Bs nearby but I got no reply at either.

In the late afternoon sunshine I meandered around the village – ever so pretty in parts – but found no other B&Bs and so, getting frustrated, I took the bull by the horns and backtracked two and a half miles to Drayton, where I made my final mistake of the day.

Riding straight past a nice-looking B&B I went for the pub option and checked in at the Red Lion. I ended up in a room measuring 7' x 9' with no chair, no television, a shower that didn't work properly (the third of those out of four, incidentally) and lots of traffic outside the window.

It wasn't even in the pub but in a separate 1970s house, at the far end of the car park, which had been converted into lots of B&B rooms. At least it was a confirmed bed for the night.

Walking down to the local shop to buy some food for tea, I received a very downhearted text from Sue, saying that the estimated cost of repairing her Clio was £500, with a ten day delay. I phoned her back and told her to go and see Ken, our friendly, local car repairer and see if he could find her something newer and better.

Having bought my evening meal, I returned to my little room, ate the food, wrote up my diary and retired to bed.

Day Mileage: 42.6 Total: 226

Wednesday, September 5th 2007.

Vale of the White Horse - Taking Chances.

The best that can be said about the Red Lion is that they served me a decent breakfast, albeit in the company of a gang of big, scruffy, cheerful labourers. I set out up the already familiar road to Steventon and there I turned west into the country lanes of the Vale of the White Horse.

A prompt start meant that I was embroiled in the morning rush hour again, even in the lanes. I noticed that the majority of cars coming towards me were driven by women between thirty and fifty, mostly with blonde hair and glasses, whose mouths were clamped grimly shut as if they were already mentally dealing with the horrors of the office.

Between East and West Hanney, the downs (formerly the Berkshire Downs but now in Oxfordshire) began to assert themselves, away to my left., I stopped to photograph West Hanney House which dominates the village and a thatcher, his pick-up loaded with thatching reeds, drove past, on his way out of the village en route to his current project, in perfect thatching weather.

By nine o'clock the traffic had died away to a trickle and peace and quiet were restored. Passing a farm in Denchworth, this peace was briefly shattered when I was treated to the clamour of synchronised egg-laying – for a few seconds the air was filled with the voices of what sounded like hundreds of squawking hens.

Fed up with the uncertainties of seeking accommodation on the hoof, I tried phoning ahead to B&B's from my internet list. Having tried seven in the Bradford-on-Avon / Melksham area and found all of them fully booked, I passed on the task to the Bradford-on-Avon Tourist Information Office, with a promise to phone them again at lunchtime.

I was about to hit the road again when I got chatting with a man out walking his dog. We found a shared interest in travel and classic cars and twenty minutes passed before, in deference to his dog and my journey, I broke it off and carried on down the road.

A mile before Uffington, I was startled to find myself being overtaken by a High Speed Train, just yards away on the other side of the hedge! The line had crept up beside me as I pedalled along and the train had contrived to arrive at a colossal rate of knots on the quarter mile stretch beside the lane just as I was passing.

White Horse Hill – with the tip of a white foot showing – and Dragon Hill.

Leaving Uffington, White Horse Hill was dead ahead and I could see hoards of people on the hill. A few hundred yards closer and it became two people and hoards of sheep!

This was the end of my flat lanes as I climbed part way up the side of the hill before turning west. Grey and overcast, it was still warm as I swooped along the undulating B4507 towards Ashbury, where Alfred the Great is reputed to have defeated the Danes in battle. I was tempted to stop for a pint at the Crown pub, which serves Arkell's Ales but it was simply too early in the day.

I was in familiar territory – the earthworks of Barbary Castle dominated the horizon ahead and in my time I have walked, cycled and flown over the whole area. My Dad, too, would have known this area well.

A climb up into Wanborough village was rewarded with a steep swoop followed by a long, very fast freewheel down the other side, bringing me to the Common Head Roundabout on the busy A419 outside Swindon... Oops! Not where I should be at all: I'd failed to hang a left in Wanborough. A quick scan of the map found a moderately easy way to retrieve the situation without the need to ride right back up the hill. Even so, it was a sharp reminder to concentrate on the business in hand.

Soon I had traversed the M4, fifth of the six motorways I had to cross, fiddled my way through Chiseldon and was heading towards Wroughton. It was now lunchtime and I could justify keeping my eyes peeled for a pub sign saying "Arkell's Ales". I planned to have my first pint in twelve years of one of my favourites – their 3Bs ale (the 3Bs being Best Bitter Beer).

Out of curiosity I took a short-cut through Overtown, a strange little place where my bell surprised three rosy cheeked, twenty-something girls walking down the middle of the road with their backs to me. They were busy chattering and oblivious to my approach until I was almost on top of them. We exchanged quick, jokey pleasantries as I passed and then I was plummeting down a steep, bumpy hill into Wroughton.

At last I was passing pubs offering all sorts of ale options, such as Wadworth's, instead of wall-to-wall Greene King. Finding an Arkell's house, the Fox & Hounds, I dismounted and was soon wrapping myself round that first pint of 3Bs in twelve years. The second pint was accompanied by a very nice Wiltshire ham salad under the inquisitive gaze of the jackdaw at the next table!

The view towards Shrivenham from near Ashbury.

House name board outside Ashbury

A brief contact with the 21st Century – M4 Junction 15.

Lunchtime companion – beside a connoisseur's sunshade!

My promised call to Bradford-on-Avon tourist information office brought details of a bed for the night in Atworth, near Melksham and on the stroke of two o'clock – the old work ethic – I left the Fox & Hounds and staggered uphill onto the Wiltshire Downs.

Passing the Science Museum storage facility on the former RAF airfield at Wroughton, I remembered that this was the scene of my best ever landing in a glider, back in the 1980s. I had flown there from our airfield at South Marston – now the Honda car factory. The only way I could tell when I was down was the sound of the wheel on the runway. Happily, the glider was a 2-seater and I had a fellow pilot, Suzy Johnstone, in the aircraft with me to witness my triumph.

Typical Wiltshire Downs scenery.

My route dropped off the Downs at Clyffe Pypard and "dropped" is the operative word – the road descends through trees at 1 in 6 with some challenging, walled bends near the bottom: very challenging if you've had two pints of Arkell's 3Bs and are doing 44.2 mph...! (as I discovered later). Fifty three years of cycling experience and the will to survive came into play. Exhilarating stuff.

Clyffe Pypard. The 1 in 6 hill is in the trees behind the cottages.

Pausing to take a photo I saw a Hercules aircraft, in full desert camouflage, on its way into Lyneham airbase. Obviously recently returned from the Middle East (or shortly to go out). A pair of Tornado fast jets, transiting through in close formation at about 1000 feet, made me think of home, where they are frequent visitors.

The Trotting Horse pub at Bushton had a unique and eye-catching porch consisting of a quarter of an enormous barrel.

It was probably the beer – a phrase sprang into my head:
"Bestriding England like the travellers of old".
And, as I told myself at the time, it do feel good.

Off to my left I could see the lighting gantries and silver tops of the hangars at Lyneham Airbase, accompanied by the sounds of several Hercules warming up and taxiing. Although they are military aircraft, as transports they are hardly weapons of war and see much more action dropping supplies to people on the ground, be they troops, refugees or starving earthquake victims.

On the run-in to Calne I had an unavoidable stretch of main road in the form of the A3102 and was not overjoyed to be back in traffic – or to see two dead badgers within 200 yards. Calne itself was a nightmare of queues and traffic jams but that was nothing compared to the nightmare of the next section of the A3102.

A mile out of Calne I passed a roadside "shrine" to a cyclist who had been killed on the road. It included a photo of the man, wearing his cycle helmet and with a big smile on his face. He looked like a really nice guy but he, I and all cyclists were let down by Wiltshire's road planners.

The A3102 is lethal for cyclists, with no verges and dense, high hedges right up to the edge of the carriageway. Consequently there is absolutely no refuge for a cyclist. You can't even fall off the bike to get out of danger. A dark blue juggernaut passed me, doing around 50 mph and about a foot from my elbow. He wouldn't wait for a gap in the oncoming traffic because he didn't want to lose momentum going uphill (I assumed).

In fairness, that was the only case of dangerous driving I encountered in sixteen days of cycling. Most drivers were courteous and careful of my safety – I saw many glance in their mirror after passing me, to make sure I was okay. As for the A3102 – I wouldn't cycle along that road again if you paid me.

Surprised to find myself alive in Melksham, I wandered along to the tourist information office to find out where I could get a cup of tea, as it was too early to go to the B&B. Not in Melksham, I was told. As an alternative, the lady suggested a short diversion to take time out at Great Chalfield Manor, a National Trust property west of the town.

Great Chalfield Manor was indeed a haven of tranquillity. Built in 1480, it is a delightful old house in a beautiful setting. The house was closed for the day but it was a joy simply to sit outside in the park and chill for a while.

Then it was time to find my way across Broughton Common to Atworth, where the tourist information office had booked my overnight accommodation. My hosts, Sean and Victoria, gave me a warm welcome and Victoria insisted on serving me tea and flapjacks before I'd even showered and changed.

So I found myself, at the theoretical halfway point in my journey, sitting in a swish armchair and steaming gently like an old locomotive at the end of the platform. I was still wearing lycra shorts and bright blue cycling vest and clutching a bone china tea-cup so delicate that the handle was too small for my man-size index finger.

I'd arranged to meet Margie, sister of Esther and Helen, for dinner and that evening we rendezvoused at the pub just along the road. Like her sisters the previous day, Margie insisted on treating me to the meal and drinks and we spent a pleasant couple of hours chatting and enjoying more good food.

Back at the digs, by the time I'd written up the diary, it was 1140 and past my bedtime.

Day mileage: 60.5   Total: 287

"To the far fields I have gone,
down along the sea
above the hills
and back again".

Rod McKuen
Fields of Wonder.

Thursday, September 6th 2007.

Into Somerset.

Waking up to a beautiful sunrise, I started my day with a splendid breakfast, including the nicest scrambled egg I've ever eaten. Victoria only charged me £30 so the £5 that should have gone to the TIC for finding her for me, plus £1 for chocolate and a bottle of spring water which both came free, went to the sponsorship fund.

Atworth was a couple of miles off the planned route, so I navigated my way through the lanes to re-join the route at Bradford-on-Avon. The morning was now overcast, despite that promising start, and the lanes were busy with the usual "rat-runners" but it was mainly a downhill ride into the Avon valley.

At Bradford-on-Avon I took a break by the Kennet & Avon Canal to soak up the atmosphere at the lock, where several boats were tied up and the waterside cafés were open. There appeared to be a more or less permanent community of canal folk and the place had really good vibrations.

Shortly before passing through Rode, I crossed the county boundary from Wiltshire into Somerset. As befits so rural a county, the sign for Somerset was decidedly overgrown.

My route took me through the centre of Frome, with the opportunity to visit a bank and do a few odd bits of shopping. As a first-time visitor, I was very impressed. The town centre is picturesque and historic and I made a note to bring Sue to stay for a weekend some time.

I arrived at coffee time and stumbled on a gem. The Garden Café, in Stony Street just off the main street, has a split level garden at the rear with one half sheltered by a canopy. The café serves locally produced, organic food and the two young ladies who served me were delightful. Genuinely interested in my ride, they were full of enthusiasm and encouragement and a joy to meet.

The canal side at Bradford-on-Avon – a pleasant spot.

As they and the proprietor were seeing me off, he pointed out that I had padlocked my bike to their three-phase electricity supply cable. I said that was so that if the lights went out, I'd know my bike and all my worldly goods were being stolen.

I bought Sue a pair of garnet ear-rings from another friendly girl in a small craft shop. On the wall she had pinned her own hand-written motto, saying "Dance as if no-one's watching". A good sentiment.

Having filled my belly and also my wallet, it was time to head out of town. My next port of call was the village of Nunney, only three miles down the road. There is a preserved Great Western Railway steam locomotive named Nunney Castle and I was keen to see the original castle.

Both village and castle were worth the stop – pretty, peaceful and unspoiled. Had it been lunchtime, the George Hotel would certainly have seen me parking the bike for a while. Built in 1373 by John de la Mare, the castle looks fairly intact at first but, like so much of our architectural heritage, it was besieged and ruined on orders from Parliament during the Civil War.

The main street at Nunney.

The Roundheads left it to fall down - but it's still there!

My lunch companion in the garden of the Lamb.

58

When I was planning the route, I had used Google Earth and spotted a super little shortcut under a dual carriageway which avoided a tricky junction and saved me half a mile of cycling (0.1% of total distance!). When I reached the spot it worked like a dream and I emerged felling very smug and pleased with myself.

I felt less smug when I rounded the next corner and was confronted with several layers of hills across my path. This was the beginning of a long stretch of "bumpy" going, when the road was seldom level or straight. It was also merely a taster for the Blackdown Hills, the first serious hills, including the highpoint of the whole journey, which I would tackle on the following day.

Throughout this end of Somerset, I kept finding myself exchanging smiles with passing motorists. Most of them were big, healthy, blonde ladies and that half second of friendly interaction was a tremendous morale booster, especially as nearly all of them were half my age! There was one exception – a blonde, tight-lipped lady with Cruella DeVille glasses, who looked at me as if I'd just crawled out of a slimy hole and was probably thinking "Look at thet chep – he obviously can't afford a car".

I put three quarters of a mile on my journey (so much for that half a mile saved earlier) by missing a turning. Purely by chance I realised my error very quickly, right by a lane that would return me to the planned route.

As the time approached one o'clock I started to watch out for a lunchtime pub. I skipped a scruffy Ushers one and then, a couple of miles later, sought guidance from a young mum walking two under-fives on ponies. She pointed me towards the Lamb at Upton Noble. Half a mile off route, it's worth the steep climb to get to it. Good, fresh food, good ale, very friendly, welcoming staff and great views from the garden. And of course, when you leave you have the fast free-wheel back down to the route.

It was only on arriving at the Lamb that I realised how humid it had been. Everything, from my helmet to my shoes, was damp or actually wet. The relative humidity must have been up around 80 per cent. The grey overcast had persisted all morning and, along with the humidity, was the downside of the long-established anti-cyclone which was keeping the rain away.

Back on the road and approaching North Brewham I passed two cheery gents pottering along the lane on fold-up bikes. I went past like an express passing a goods train, exchanging greetings as I did so.

Shortly after going through Bruton, I missed my second turning of the day. This mistake spat me out onto an A-road and actually saved me the three quarters of a mile I'd wasted earlier. It also spared me the complexities of Castle Cary and, as I was now in crack on mode, I didn't mind at all. The terrain was flat and, riding beside a railway line, I was going like a train.

At Lydford-on-Fosse I recognised the Cross Keys, where my son Andy, my Mum and I had a meal while on holiday about ten years earlier. At the same time I crossed the Fosse Way, an historic route for earlier cross-country travellers in ancient times.

The thought crossed my mind that I must be as close as I was going to get to Glastonbury Tor. No sooner had I thought it than I cleared the end of a hedge and there, through the murk, was the Tor.

Re-joining the road after stopping to photograph the Tor I met up with a fellow cyclist, who stayed with me for several miles into Somerton. He had cycled from Land's End to John O'Groats in May but had done it entirely on main roads.

We parted company at Somerton as he needed to crack on at a faster pace, being on an unladen racing bike, and considerably younger than me. Suddenly *I* was the goods train! I skipped Somerton, self proclaimed Royal Capital of Ancient Wessex, as all I wanted at this stage was to reach Langport for a shower and a nice cup of tea.

It was only four miles to Langport, which I soon rattled off, and in no time I was wheeling the bike *through the hotel lounges* to get it to the yard where it would be stored. And would you believe it – half an hour after I checked in, the sun finally came out and the clouds cleared away entirely. After dinner I took a stroll around the town and took a few photographs as the light faded.

Glastonbury Tor – not how the tourist brochures show it...

The Langport Arms Hotel.

61

Langport High Street at Dusk.

A rather splendid clothes drier for my cycling mitts.

Back at the hotel I seized the opportunity to wash various bits and pieces, wrote up the diary and had a well-earned drink in the bar before hitting the sack.

Day mileage: 52.8   Total: 340.

Friday, September 7th 2007.

Over The Top.

On the previous day, despite the overcast, I had caught a bit of sunburn so before leaving Langport I bought and applied some sunscreen.

Twenty five years after I had last visited the town, I was expecting a flat start to my day but no – the road to Curry Rivel follows the only available hill. My escape from that main road was a B-road which wasn't signposted, so I missed the turning. I may have been guided by angels, as I found myself passing a teleflorist's. Naturally, I called in to send some flowers to Sue.

The map showed an easy way back to my pink line, so no damage done. At the gate to an elevated cornfield I paused to make phone calls to Sue (not mentioning the impending flowers) and to my friend Mick, whom I was hoping to meet for lunch.

Back on the bike a fortuitous sign drew my attention to the junction where I needed to leave the B-road, otherwise that would have been another turning missed. Now that I was fully fit I was getting too relaxed and just trolleying along enjoying the scenery.

The scenery this morning had an edge – the Blackdown Hills spread ever larger across my path. Initially, their effect was barely noticeable: I just became aware that I was gently gaining height most of the time. Then came Broadway and Broadway Pound and, all at once, the gradient became more pronounced.

Not sure if I was on the right lane, I spent at least ten minutes trying to find out from an elderly gent who was trimming his garden hedge. He'd never heard of Holman Clavel, where I'd arranged to meet Mick for lunch, and didn't even know the road layout in his local area. He was so keen to talk that I suspect he was a lonely widower. He was a gentleman, anyway.

I soon found another gent who confirmed that I had strayed slightly, but it didn't matter as he said that all the lanes ended up at the same place and that, whichever one I took, I had a lot of hard work ahead of me!

And so I started the serious climb, knowing that I had to gain a thousand feet above sea level – which is where I'd started that morning – under a cloudless sky with rising temperatures. I was given a brief respite higher up the lane when the way was blocked by a truck offloading builder's materials. That five or six minute break enabled me to regain my breath and cool down under a tree without having to admit that I needed to do so.

Then there was no escape and I went up and up and up. At one point I walked for a quarter of a mile because I was too hot to keep pedalling furiously in bottom gear and walking was actually faster. There were all sorts of little, inter-connecting lanes, with no signage of any kind, and I was glad of my foresight in buying a bell that incorporated a compass, which kept me roughly on track.

The theory that all roads lead to Rome eventually held good and I could prove that I was back on track. I was also on top of the Blackdown Hills, Staple Hill to be precise.

I found the pub without too much trouble and discovered why I had seen no signs to guide me – despite appearing on the road maps, Holman Clavel actually consisted of just the pub!

I was three quarters of an hour early, so I sat in the shade of a beech tree and caught up with communications until Mick arrived. A passing cyclist saw me and asked if I was okay. When I said I was waiting for a mate to come and buy me a pint, he called over his shoulder "That's more than okay!"

When Mick turned up we discovered what a good pub it was. Like the Lamb, the previous day's lunch stop, they were very friendly, serving excellent food and well-kept ales. We sat in the pub yard, enjoyed our ale and caught up on the news. I think Mick was quite impressed with my set-up and possibly a little envious.

Incidentally at 2.18, whilst sat in the sunshine with Mick, digesting lunch and with 360 miles on the clock, I completed the first week of the journey. When we departed, the landlady filled my drink bottle with orange squash and like other kind souls along the way, wouldn't accept payment.

Staple Hill – at 1,000 ft, the highest point on the whole journey.

A couple of old-timers – over the hill but not dead!

Before setting off, I phoned ahead to try and tie up that night's accommodation. The George at Uffculme sounded promising but when my call was answered, a rural, Zummerzet voice told me that the landlady was out until 4.00 o'clock, so I said I'd ring back. Leaving Mick to his short drive home, I headed west once more.

Having carefully planned most of the route to minimise hill-climbing, I had opted to go over the Blackdown Hills to avoid lots of main road work as well as the nightmare of going through Taunton. The road along the top is lined with trees so, with no distant views, it was easy to forget how high I was.

Along the road I passed the sign for Quants Moor, a National Trust picnic area and viewpoint. Curiosity got the better of me and I rode in to take a look.

Suddenly I was very aware of my altitude, looking down on the M5, a few miles away, and across to the southern slopes of the Quantock Hills. This was good news – Uffculme was down in the valley, so there must be lots of free, downhill miles to come.

Looking out over the valley from Quants Moor.

These four snails were living several feet up on a cow parsley.

Half a mile up the road I detoured along a woodland path to reach the Wellington Memorial, which I'd seen many times from the M5 without realising that it is three sided. For several years it has been fenced off around the base, due to structural instability and the danger of falling masonry. It is still a hugely impressive edifice.

Returning to the road, I left Somerset and was welcomed into Devon with a swift, exhilarating, two mile freewheel down off the ridge into Hemyock.

Another phone call to the George Inn at Uffculme brought good news: the landlady, Val, answered and said "Yes, there *is* room at the inn!" and I liked her before I'd even met her.

The Wellington Memorial from the Culme Valley.

It was four miles through pretty Devon countryside to Uffculme and as soon as I walked into the bar at the George, Val greeted me like an old friend. She had only taken over the pub six months earlier and was in the early stages of an ambitious renovation project. At £25 this was my cheapest stay of the whole trip. I would discover why later.

Val showed me the way up to my tiny room, one of three in the newly created first floor – formerly the loft – of the main building. The sloping ceiling led down to a small window at knee height which I could only reach by lying on the bed. I had to dip my head even to stand near the door. There were no facilities whatsoever – not even a chair – apart from a television which didn't work.

This was my only "non" en-suite room and the bathroom was at the far end of the corridor, yet I was happy enough. Perhaps it was the afterglow of the lunchtime beer. The only shower was in the bath so I made do with a sit-down shower, got changed and lay on the bed to write up the diary.

Through my binoculars I watched a ploughman finishing off his day's work turning over a sloping, hillside field of stubble a couple of miles away, across the valley.

Dinner was adequate but not spectacular and afterwards I settled down with Val and the locals to watch Argentina trounce France in the opening match of the Rugby World Cup.

Before I retired for the night, Val said "If you want to make an early start in the morning, there's everything you need on the landing – bread, a toaster, tea, milk and so on." I said I wouldn't start that early but she said "Well, in case you do, just unlock the door downstairs and let yourself out of the gate". I thought no more about it and went up to my tiny room to bed.

Day mileage: 33.5   Total: 373.

Down to Gehenna or up to the Throne,
He travels fastest who travels alone.
Rudyard Kipling.

Saturday, September 8th 2007.

The Best of Devon.

Well, the George Inn wasn't really offering B&B – just B! There was no breakfast apart from the do-it-yourself kit on the landing. In the morning, at around 8.30, I wandered downstairs, unlocked the door into the pub yard to get a breath of fresh air and enjoy the bright sunshine for half an hour.

There was no sign of life anywhere in the pub so, eventually, I gave up, packed my things, loaded the bike and left. It was as if Val knew that would be the situation beforehand. Weird.

Fortunately, two doors down the road was the Post Office, where I bought some food and drink and set myself up for the day. A mile out of town I stopped in a field entrance for an impromptu, sunlit breakfast of ham salad sandwiches and orange juice.

A further two miles and I was able to mentally tick off the last of the six motorways I had to cross – the M5, which had been in the background since the previous afternoon. It was possibly the busiest, though the M4 would give it a run for its money. Once again I had a reminder of the hectic world I was carefully avoiding.

Feeling quite superior with my zero carbon footprint, I carried on into Cullompton, where I ran head-on into the Twenty-first Century. It's a lovely little town but was frantic with local and through traffic. I suppose I should have made allowances for the fact that it was Saturday morning but, after a visit to a bank ATM, I hopped back on the bike and skedaddled.

At the edge of town I turned off onto the lane leading to Bradninch and amused myself by nipping the growing points out of brambles in the roadside hedges. Over many years I've perfected my technique to the point where I'm successful, even at fairly high speeds. Going slowly, you just keep your eye on the shoot and pinch it as you reach it. At 20 mph, you pinch thin air a good foot ahead of the bramble and the reaction time of finger and thumb results in a triple meeting at the critical point – if your luck's in... A high priority is to avoid wild roses, which have a passing resemblance to a bramble but take the tip off *your finger!*

I began to notice that junctions, even between tiny lanes, had names. All were crosses with names like Clapper Cross, Redyeates Cross, Clannaborough Cross, Parsonage Cross and so on. Each signpost is marked with the name plus a small cross symbol.

The signpost for Stumpy Cross.

These crosses are really useful and are named on the map, so they enable one to pinpoint one's location precisely in a maze of small roads and lanes. I'm surprised the idea hasn't been adopted elsewhere.

At Red Cross, I took a breather to turn the map over, admire the view and have a drink before sending a couple of texts. I suddenly noticed a trickle of blood down my left forearm that was threatening to drip. I got a serviette, thieved from the previous day's pub, and mopped it up to find the tiniest pinprick. Some small predator had used a bucketful of anti-coagulant and caused me to leak like a sieve. A quick dab of spit restored things to normal.

Just as I was sorted and reaching for the map, a car came round the junction and drew up beside me. The young lady driver opened her window and asked me if I was alright. She had been driving past when her daughter – aged about six – said "Mummy, that man's bleeding badly". So she had turned round farther up the road and came all the way back to see if she could help. Hardly had she been reassured, thanked and gone, when a very pretty girl on a mountain bike pulled up.

She was out for a local ride for a few hours and stayed to chat for a good ten minutes. My spirits were lifted no end. When she discovered that I was cycling for charity, she reached for her purse to give me some money but found she'd left it at home. At her suggestion, I gave her my card so that she could post me a cheque but she either lost the card or didn't get round to it because nothing ever turned up.

There are a lot of lovely ladies in Somerset and Devon.

Crossing a river, I was astonished to realise that it was the River Exe, on its way to Exeter and the sea. (Looking at the picture of Stumpy Cross on the previous page, showing Exeter 7 miles away, I should have been less surprised than I was).

It was like two different rivers – upstream of the bridge it was a placid, country river, not unlike the upper Thames, with big clumps of Himalayan Balsam. Below the bridge it turned into a concrete-sided channel leading to a straight weir, over which it dropped about a foot and became a busy river, more like the Wye, with ripples, waves and eddies.

The River Exe, looking upstream...

...and downstream.

The Thorverton Arms at – where else? – Thorverton, loomed over my horizon just as my stomach started sending urgent messages about lunch. My first pint of Otter Ale in many years went down a treat, as did the second one, accompanied by a really nice ploughman's platter and the chattering of busy jackdaws.

The view from the front of the Thorverton Arms.

As the swallows gathered in preparation for the journey south, the wagtails had arrived from the north – a pair performed a little dance on the roof of the pub.

The front row of the grid – in Thorverton's main street.

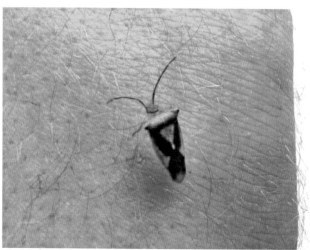

A new friend who arrived on my left knee while I was taking the photo above.

Passing through a steady succession of villages and small towns, it was noticeable, not to mention encouraging, to see how many sub-Post Offices are surviving and working hard to ensure that they continue to do so. The favourite strategy is to become an all-singing, all-dancing, friendly village store where they can sell you almost anything and if they haven't got it, they can get it. They also become the place where paths cross, news and gossip are exchanged and people keep in touch the old fashioned way.

Between Thorverton and Crediton, I passed *through* a badger sett. Both banks of the road were riddled with holes. I wonder if they linked up below the road – knowing what prodigious burrowers badgers are, I wouldn't be at all surprised. At least living by the roadside would keep them safe from the attention of badger baiters.

In Crediton I found a good cycle shop and went in to buy a new pair of pedals. I had become increasingly concerned about the way the left one, in particular, creaked when climbing hills and I certainly didn't want it to pack up miles from anywhere.

Super-embarrassment when the guy in the shop found that the pedals were fine but both cranks needed tightening! I had replaced the chainset a couple of weeks before starting this epic and the instructions were quite specific – re-tighten after a week. And did I remember...?

Chastened, I moved on up the road to the Tourist Information Office to seek some overnight accommodation. There I met Katherine, a delightful, helpful girl, who spent ages phoning around and being told the usual story: "No vacancies". Last chance saloon was a lady called Lesley, who works part-time at the TIC, and she came up trumps. So, equipped with directions, I set off to meet Lesley.

Lesley's house, Harebell, was at Copplestone, four miles west of Crediton and about a mile off my route. On my way there, I saw and photographed my last swallows of 2007, gathered on power wires and – looking at the photograph – facing north... Not the right way for Africa but I expect they were facing into the wind which, once they embarked on their journey, would be helping them along.

A solitary church across the fields.

Hardy cyclamen on the roadside opposite Harebell.

I arrived at Harebell hot, weary and grubby but Lesley made me very welcome. My room was a dramatic change from the previous night's accommodation and all that I could have wished for: beautiful decoration and furnishings, lots of space, everything worked and nothing was too much trouble.

The garden was beautiful and extensive and I was instructed to treat it as my own. After a shower and change of clothes, I took her at her word and went down to explore. Lesley introduced me to her old horse, Bella, who was 37 years old and still bright as a button, if a little arthritic and cantankerous. She came and said hello but soon lost interest in me when Lesley arrived, bringing her evening meal.

I had dinner at the 650 year-old New(!) Inn at Coleford, a mile down the lane. Lesley offered husband Ken to chauffeur me down there and collect me when summoned but I said I'd enjoy the walk. Dinner was very nice – if not cheap – and was accompanied by a pint of Skinners Honey Ale and one of Otter Ale.

I was glad of my decision to stagger (uphill) back from the pub as there was a delightful afterglow in the western sky. I stopped a couple of times in field gateways to enjoy the changing light on a hint of mist in the tranquil valley below. The only sounds were the last rooks of the day exchanging greetings with the night's first owl.

Back at Harebell, I phoned ahead to the White Hart Hotel in Launceston and booked a room for the following two nights. This would give me a carefree run for the following day plus the bonus of a day off in Launceston to sightsee, have a haircut and get some clothes cleaned.

Before retiring for the night, I sat at a very elegant dressing table to write up the diary, have a look on the map at the next day's route and swap texts with Sue. As I did so, I had a cup of drinking chocolate and luxuriated in the spacious, civilised surroundings.

The New Inn at Coleford.

Dusk, photographed walking back up the hill, under the affluence of incohol.

Day mileage: 26.5   Total: 399

Sunday, 9th September 2007

Across the Tamar.

I woke early, made myself a cup of tea and sat by the open window, just soaking up the view and listening to the wildlife. Prominent amongst the birds were the local ravens – a familiar sound as we have them in the woods at home. The unmistakeable honking of geese gradually asserted itself above the other sounds and I grabbed the camera just in time as around seventy of them flew over in a giant arc across the morning sky.

My early morning flypast.

At breakfast I finally met Lesley's husband, Ken – a lovely guy, as straight as they come. The three of us chatted for ages about all manner of things. They lost a son in a motorcycling accident and obviously still feel the loss very deeply. They have a beautiful, original oil painting in the Impressionist style, which they bought in his memory and Lesley always keeps a vase of fresh flowers in front of it.

When it was time to leave, they both came out to see me on my way down the lane – a pair of lovely, quiet, gentle people.

A few miles down the road I crossed the Coast-to-Coast long-distance path. Across the West Country peninsular, that is, not across England, so long*ish...* And soon after that I saw either my geese again – in which case they had been flying around for several hours – or another group of similar size.

I briefly joined the A3072 to pass through the village of Bow, before turning north, into a small, rather unkempt lane. The lane resumed the required westerly direction after half a mile or so and began a long, gentle ascent onto a ridge with good views to either side and clumps of montbretia flowers along the verge in places.

Once up on the ridge, I stopped to take a refreshment break and remove my jersey, having got quite warm on the climb. I was greatly covetous of a pile of rounds of beech wood, recently cut, which would have been splendid to store and season for carving.

At Staddon Moor Cross, I turned left and began a long, fast glide into North Tawton, where I stopped to take advantage of an open shop (it being Sunday) and buy some lunch. It's a town which is interesting, rather than beautiful and, judging from some of the buildings, it has a fascinating past. (I now know that there was a Roman fort there, probably built on the site of an ancient Druidic sanctuary in attempt to stifle the native, Celtic religion).

The previous day, the front gear changer had messed me about going up a particularly steep slope. It refused to change onto the small chain ring, causing me to stall and abandon ship in a hurry to avoid falling off. Peeved and frustrated, I had kicked it in an endeavour to give it the extra millimetre of travel that it needed. Naturally that made it more cantankerous than ever, rather than improving anything.

On the quiet lane out of North Tawton I gave in and did what I should have done in the first place – get the tools out, straighten it all out and do the necessary fine adjustment. Consequently, the second half of the day flowed much more smoothly.

As I drew nearer to Okehampton, the great mass of Dartmoor, off to my left like most of the hills so far on my journey, made me awfully pleased that I was circumnavigating it rather than crossing over it, as some pundits had suggested from the comfort of their armchairs.

The cyclists dream – downhill ahead.   The road to North Tawton.

Late Summer in England – and the harvest has obviously been gathered in.

Reaching Okehampton I went to visit the Museum of Dartmoor Life, only to find it closed. However, there was an outside courtyard containing various exhibits and a café – also closed. I took a few photos and then settled at a picnic table *["This table is only for the use of patrons of the Victorian Pantry Tearooms"]*.

Lunch consisted of two mini-pork pies, a bag of crisps, and a Yorkie bar washed down with a generous measure of Raspberry and Cranberry Ribena ("Full of anti-oxidants"). Happily the toilets were open, probably because the Dartmoor Way passes smack through the museum courtyard.

Three miles outside Okehampton my little lane tip-toed through the noisy complexities of the major junction of the A30 and the A386. I needed to join the main road traffic for a hundred yards of ducking and diving but the drivers were, as ever, considerate of my undoubted vulnerability and helped me across their path to escape into the back roads again.

This back road was the Old Road – an earlier incarnation of the A30 – and, being a former trunk road, had no serious gradients, an excellent surface and next to no traffic. A big plus. Every now and then a pair of 1950s British motor-bikes would potter past: evidence of a rally somewhere around.

Soon I encountered my first pair of long-distance cyclists heading away from Land's End and, sure enough, they were en-route for John O'Groats. I wished them good luck. By the time I reached Lewdown, I had met seven, all with that same huge challenge ahead of them. Suddenly my own journey seemed less epic.

I kept getting glimpses, off to my left, of an intriguing, hill-top tower on the edge of Dartmoor, I took a couple of photos, despite the dreadful light. Subsequent investigation revealed it to be the famous Brent Tor, of which I'd heard many times but which I'd never seen.

The museum was closed but the welcome still came with a smile!

I took this picture simply because these were the brightest colours I had seen all day – honestly!

Brent Tor. You can see how flat and grey the sky was.

None too soon I could see Launceston on its hill ahead of me and there was the River Tamar, with the bridge which would carry me into Cornwall. As ever, I paused to photograph the county sign and was hit by an emotional jolt as it suddenly dawned on me that I was actually going to do this thing. On the journey, one tends to be preoccupied with the view over the hedge, the next corner, the next hill, the next town and the next overnight stop. The bigger picture tends to fade into irrelevance. All at once my ultimate destination – still nearly 100 miles away – demanded my attention.

I entered Launceston by the South Gate but, before I did so, there was the small matter of afternoon tea. Nestling at the side of the gate was a small café which appeared to be in total darkness. The sign in the window said "Open", so I tried the door. It was indeed open, so I parked the bike, removed gloves and helmet, smoothed my hair, which contorts into interesting shapes in the helmet's ventilation gaps, and entered.

Inside I was welcomed by the strains of Classic FM wafting through the place. The proprietor was in the very back of the café, clearing up. The café closed at 2.00; this was 4.30. The proprietor was Irish. "Dat's no problem at all" he said "What'll you be having?" What could I ask for, two miles into Cornwall, but a cream tea! And he served it up. And it was delicious. Just as well – I'd come a long way for it (and certainly hadn't expected it to be served up by an Irishman!).

From there it was up and around the corner to the White Hart Hotel, where the receptionist was very welcoming and arranged to stash the bike in the hotel laundry. After that it was the standard procedure: up to the room, throw the kit off and get into the shower.

Day mileage: 33.5   Total: 433

"The World is a book.

He who does not travel reads only one page".

St Augustine.

The South Gate, last survivor of Launceston's four gates. To its right, hidden among the flowers, is the little café run by a fascinating Irishman where I stopped for the mandatory Cornish cream tea.

A Day Off.

This was rest and re-boot day. I needed a haircut and also needed to have my one decent "non-cycling" shirt properly cleaned and pressed. I asked at reception where I could get this done and the only place she could think of was the laundry which did the hotel's washing.

When I found the laundry, the lady there said the only way she could do it was to put it through as a "Same Day Special" and that it would be £8.00! With only the one day available I bit the bullet and gave her the shirt. Later, fifty yards down the street from the front door of the hotel, I was to find a specialist shirt cleaners: "Have your shirt cleaned and pressed in an hour – only £2.99". Ah well.

The White Hart Hotel – the sign says it all.

The haircut was a brisk affair – a young girl with a lot of black eye make-up whisked around my head in no time, even trimming my ears (See Billy Connolly on ear and nostril hair!), doing a very fair job and chattering away while she did it.

Lighter and cooler, I set out to explore Launceston. I took photos of the castle from every corner of the town and then went inside and climbed to the top of the keep to look back at the town.

Launceston Castle as it was...

...and as it is now.

A well-kept back garden, spotted from the Castle.

A ridge-soaring buzzard with Dartmoor in the background haze.

91

Returning to the interesting Irishman's café at the South Gate for a cup of coffee, I spent a pleasant twenty minutes chatting to a couple of Geordie bikers who were doing things the easy way, on motorbikes. When they left, I chatted for a while to the proprietor, with a background of Classic FM again.

I said I thought that the White Hart was a hotel in decline, to which he replied that Launceston was a town in decline and maybe Cornwall was a county in decline. He felt that Devon was on the up and the Royal Duchy was on the slide.

I bought, wrote and posted cards to family and close friends, explored some more and had lunch at a small café, hidden away in a back street. Returning to the hotel, I booked accommodation ahead for the rest of the tour, removing the pressure of uncertainty but also tying myself to a schedule.

A whole string of phone calls and texts followed as I reported progress to those left behind and made arrangements to meet friends Roger and Jeannette a couple of days along the road ahead.

Having been disappointed by the previous evening's hotel dinner, and having had a decent lunch, I popped out and bought some bits and pieces for my evening meal. There followed a picnic tea in the room, in front of the television.

I discovered that my handlebar computer, fount of all statistics, having no work to do all day had decided to dump all data and reset itself to factory default settings. Fortunately I was one step ahead of it and had enough noted down to re-write everything back into it (having thoughtfully brought the instructions with me).

Before hitting the sack, I wandered down to the bar and had a pint of fizzy ale while watching the huge TV at the end of the room. It felt strange not to have been pedalling all day.

Day mileage: 0!   Total: Still 433!

Tuesday, 11th September 2007

West to the Atlantic Ocean.

Launceston being on a hill, I covered the first half mile of the day without turning a pedal – just sat on the bike, pointed it down hill and let the brake off. I seem to have been blessed with lots of easy starts to my days but the rest of Cornwall was to change this.

Leaving town I passed the Launceston Steam Railway and stopped to take some photos. It was a scrappy, disorganised place but the one locomotive there seemed to be well cared for.

It was nice to be back on quiet, country lanes as I headed due west into the sun dappled Cornish valleys. In the first mile or two I met several locals walking their dogs and exchanged greetings with each of them as I passed.

Two miles along the lane I had a little reminder about safety when I scooted down a small, steep descent with dark shadow at the bottom. I realised just in time that, in the shadow, lurked a sharp left-hand bend and I rocketed round it, just managing to keep to the correct side of the road. Coming the other way was a large, silver 1950s car, also keeping to *his* correct side of the road. We passed safely but, especially in that narrow lane, if either of us had transgressed even a little, the result would have been disaster.

Near Treneglos I met two young girl cyclists who were on their way to John O'Groats. We stopped, compared notes and took each other's photos. Then we wished each other God speed and continued on our separate ways.

I wish I'd got their names. I'd like to know how they got on and if they made it. They looked so young and vulnerable when one considered what they had taken on. Mind you, they probably thought I was a brave old man. All things are relative and the world looks different from differing perspectives.

Farther along I came to the A395, which offered a flat, direct route to Davidstow – where the cheese comes from – and Camelford. But sticking to principles, I opted for the bumpy way, keeping to the byways and lanes and so crossed straight over.

The Launceston Steam Railway.

En-route for the top of Scotland – I hope they made it safely.

Before dropping into the steep valley of the tiny River Inny, I took a drink break in a field gateway and suddenly became aware of Bodmin Moor, sprawled across the southern horizon, looking most imposing. It held no terrors for me as once again, my carefully planned route took me safely around the side.

The view over Abbott's Hendra to Bodmin Moor.

The lane through the valley, while putting an extra mile and a lot of up-and-down on my journey, was very pretty and the river was a bubbling, burbling joy. I leaned on the parapet of the old, stone bridge over the Inny and watched small birds prospecting for insects around the edge of the river as it tumbled over the rocks.

Perfect peace, with no sounds of the rest of the world, traffic, aircraft, other people's mobile phones or anything. I wondered if the two girls had come that way and seen it – they may well have done, as they seem to have adopted the same policy of using small, quiet roads and avoiding traffic.

The River Inny tumbling over a rock ledge.

I started to pass posters saying "No more wind farms in North Cornwall". Then I spotted a planning application notice for four wind generators "not exceeding 120 metres in height". That's four hundred feet in old money, which is enormous. I could see why they were opposing them.

At Davidstow I re-crossed the A395, then the A39 and headed west along another pretty lane where, 451 miles form Lowestoft Ness, I caught my first glimpse of the Atlantic Ocean. Sadly it was too hazy to show up in a photograph but there it was; another milestone on my long and winding road.

I've no idea what this was, other than the first standing stone I saw in Cornwall.

Montbretia: as in southwest Ireland, Cornish hedgerows are so much nicer...

Leaving the planned route (again!) I sacrificed an enormous amount of height to make my first ever visit to legendary Tintagel. The swoop down into the town was refreshing and exhilarating, and at some point I reached 36.4 m.p.h. Consequently it didn't take long.

The road down to...

I stopped at the first decent pub and ordered a real, local pasty, with chips, and a pint of St Austell Tribute, as previously enjoyed at the Lion at Waddesdon and the George at Clifton Hampden. Then, relaxing in the pub garden, I breathed the sea air and enjoyed lunch in the sunshine.

Tintagel Castle and the surrounding ruins would be a magical, mystical place were it not for us tourists. It seems to be a magnet for obese people, waddling around and setting out on the formidable walk down to the sea and back up to the castle. In the tourist season I should think they deal with a heart attack a week.

Now came the balancing of the books. It was time to pay the price for that glorious rush down the hill. I was 800' below where I should be and so, as the song says, "The Only Way is Up". The up was pretty in places but there was an awful lot of it, sometimes causing me to dismount and walk. Eventually, more than a little warm, I reached the top and rejoined the route, enjoying a long freewheel which soon dried me out and restored weary legs.

My overnight stop was two miles off route and involved another dizzy dive, reaching 37.2 m.p.h., back to sea level once again. The village of Port Isaac was as picturesque as my hotel was bizarre!

I was staying at The Old Schoolhouse which is indeed a converted school, built in 1843. In a strange, trendy attempt to recapture the atmosphere of a Victorian school, they had spent huge sums of money on arty-farty special effects but cut equally huge corners on basic fittings and facilities.

The clothes rail in the wardrobe was too short, so they had threaded a piece of copper water pipe over one end of it to extend it. Meanwhile the actual heating pipes were hanging in mid-air in front of the skirting board because their clips hadn't been properly fitted and had come adrift.

Above the bed pillows floated a "halo of light" made of Christmas lights, arranged around a wheel rim so that, when making love, one's lover's head would be framed with a circle of 40 or so 0.75 watt "stars". However, the romantic effect would be somewhat diminished by the need to get out of bed after this memorable, magical moment in order to unplug the lights from the wall...

The plain, flat room door had been painted with planks and a wood-framed blackboard bearing fire precaution information. It was very realistic and must have cost a fortune to create. A real, second hand door would have been cheaper and just as effective. Perhaps I'm a heathen and don't appreciate art...

The room itself was clean, the bed was very comfortable and the view from the window, overlooking the harbour, was sensational. It needed to be – this was the most expensive stay of my whole journey.

This is a completely flat door. Only the handle is real.

In the event of a
FIRE

1. Raise the alarm using the 'Break Glass' alarm located outside your room in the hallway.

2. Fire extinguishers can be located in all the hallways.

If you hear the fire alarm:

1. Evacuate the building quickly and calmly.

2. Do not pack away or attempt to take your belongings.

3. Assemble in the car park.

Notice, frame, screws, "planks", shadows – everything is hand painted.

The "halo" of lights above the bed. The trailing wire wandered off across the room to a wall socket!

Port Isaac Harbour viewed from outside the Old Schoolhouse...

...and the Old Schoolhouse (centre) viewed across the harbour.

The Golden Lion pub was serious about seeing off the excise men...

I went to explore down by the harbour, amongst the last of the day's visitors. Apparently these first two weeks of September are known in the accommodation trade as the "Blue Rinse" weeks. This is when we pensioners and retired folk come out of the woodwork and go on holiday, after the kids have gone back to school. Certainly, most of the trippers were the "senior" side of 60.

Looking down towards the harbour.

It was a peaceful evening with the water just lapping onto the slipway and hardly any activity on the part of the local fishermen. Even the gulls were sitting quietly, surveying the passing scene, which consisted mostly of couples and small groups wandering rather aimlessly as they "did" Port Isaac.

I had arranged to meet my friends Jeannette and Roger, from Falmouth, for dinner and they duly turned up and whisked me off in their car to a friendly pub, where we enjoyed a good meal and a chat. Then, another early night and the sleep of the just.

Day mileage: 32.4   Total: 465

Four Visits to the Sea

My early night meant that I awoke early too, so I took a stroll around Port Isaac and down to the harbour. The village was delightfully free of other tourists and the only people I saw were a few fishermen, a couple of locals walking their dogs and a friendly dustman.

Early morning tranquillity in Port Isaac.

Seeing the village without the crowds brought home to me what a trial they must be for the locals, even if they are its main source of income. Pottering around and peeking into odd corners, I started to get a feeling of how things must have been before the days of mass tourism.

I wished Sue could have been with me – it would have been her idea of heaven, being by the sea with a clear blue sky, peace and quiet and just the odd gull on a chimney pot saying "Hah hah hah".

The village fishermen's base.

Locally sourced decoration in a doorway.

I mentioned earlier that I often had an easy, downhill start to my day. Cornwall – apart from Launceston – was to change all that, starting today! Straight from the front of the hotel, I was standing up on the pedals and slogging uphill to regain the height that I'd sacrificed to stay at Port Isaac.

I joked about the topography with a friendly local lady walking a small dog, as I puffed past her. Little did I realise that hers was to be one of very few friendly faces I would see for the next couple of hours. For some reason, on this morning, the majority of people I greeted, carefully didn't look and pretended not to have heard me. Happily this was unusual – most people were only too happy to return my greeting. Perhaps I simply picked the wrong ones.

At the top of the road and back on my route, I continued to gain height for several, miles of easy ascent. Then I began an equally gentle descent towards Rock, where I would board the Padstow ferry.

On the road into Rock I had a wondrous view across the estuary of the River Camel as the tide raced out, stealthily stranding moored boats on sandbanks. On the far side, Padstow nestled under its brim of trees in the sunshine, looking very picturesque yet also quite important with its harbour and slipway.

Boats moored in the Camel estuary.

The morning light on Padstow.

There was no jetty for the ferry at Rock, just a queue on the beach. Eventually the ferry appeared on the far side, being carried towards the sea by the ebbing tide. It made a huge sweeping curve to our side of the river and started working against the current.

The helmsman was working the engine hard and yet the craft was barely making progress towards us. Once it reached us, though, he made it look like parking in a supermarket car park – he just arrived, swung the boat round, lowered the ramp and there he was. Skill born of years of practise.

On the ferry I chatted to a young couple with two kids. It turned out that the husband was a keen cyclist and, surveying the bike, he said "You've got the right tyres there – cast iron, they are – never get a puncture," which was reassuring.

Approaching the Padstow side of the estuary the helmsman was in some doubt as to whether he would be able to get us ashore at the landing point nearer to Padstow, because of the falling water level. He made one attempt and failed but tried again nearby and succeeded. He hustled us all ashore, rapidly embarked the waiting passengers and beat a hasty retreat. Until the tide returned, he would be using a landing point half a mile nearer the sea.

The beach where we landed was west of the town and at the foot of a long flight of steps which led up to a park, where cycling was forbidden. Having carried my fully loaded bike up the steps and walked through the park, I entered Padstow which, thanks to Rick Stein, if one believes the locals, was jammed with pedestrians.

There were people everywhere, seemingly all carrying plastic buckets and spades in every fluorescent shade of the rainbow, most wandering vacantly and filling the road. It was impossible to ride the bike so I walked some more until I could escape up a side street and head for the hills. As I was back at sea level, out meant up but, since I was still fairly fresh, this was no problem. It was a relief to be back in open country and on my own. "Padstein" was hell on earth.

Having circumnavigated R.A.F. St Mawgan, where the Nimrod jets are based, I had a nostalgic moment when I passed the sign to Mawgan Porth. My younger brother, Steve, and his wife Julia, who both died in their 40s from cancer, within a year of each other, used to go there most years on holiday. I pictured them in their orange MG Midget, turning into that road and looking forward to a reviving cup of tea after the journey from Berkshire.

The last passengers for Rock hurry aboard at Padstow beach to beat the receding tide.

The view back to Rock from the top of the steps at Padstow.

After a while I saw another wind farm of sixteen turbines, the height of which I estimated at 120 feet. This was stunning when I remembered that the application notice I had seen the previous day had specified a maximum height of 120 metres – more than three times the size of these.

From this point on, I was seldom out of sight of a wind farm – nearly all of the same design, with sixteen 120 foot turbines. I began to understand the campaigners' demands for no more.

It was approaching lunchtime when I came to St Columb Major but, not seeing an appealing pub, I decided to press on. Only a mile or two later I started to feel the pangs of hunger as my body used up the last of breakfast. Soon I found myself running out of steam on moderate hills and having to dismount and walk.

Time to break out the Dextrosol sweets: a source of rapidly available energy brought along for precisely this situation. Two of them propelled me to Newlyn East, where I found the Pheasant Inn, conveniently situated right on the side of the road. I sat outside and enjoyed a three cheese ploughman's lunch and two pints of St Austell Tribute Ale with the pub's friendly, black cat for company.

With hindsight and remembering how quickly I sank the first pint, part of the morning's problem may have been de-hydration. I had used very little water all morning. Another lapse became apparent at the pub – I'd been in such a hurry to escape the nightmare of Padstow that I'd forgotten to top up either my wallet or my mobile phone card.

This left me with a predicament, as there were no more towns on the route to Portreath apart from Goonhavern. When that failed to provide a solution to either problem, the answer was simple. I left my planned route and took a cooling, death-defying plunge down into Perranporth.

More crowds shuffling around, more plastic spades, Lloyds TSB was opposite a store where I could top up my phone card, as well as take on board a few snacks for the journey. So I had a solution to my two problems and the creation of a new one. Yup- I was back at sea-level and would have to climb again.

Heading out of town, I passed a guy with a pack on his back, pretty obviously walking to Land's End – BAREFOOT. Was this courage, folly or religious conviction? And where had he started from? I guess he had his reasons; in fact he probably had a very interesting tale to tell.

A corner of one of the ubiquitous wind farms.

My lunch companion.

Beauty on the side of a Cornish lane.

I fiddled and switchbacked my way around the lanes to the east of St Agnes and found myself passing Goonbell Stables, where, in 1979, I first ever sat my bum on a horse. Her name was Starlight and she had a loose shoe which rattled when walking or trotting on the road.

Near Mawla, having just rejoined the pink line, I immediately strayed off it again. Stopping at a junction to peruse the map and try to retrieve the situation, I met a delightful Cornish lady on her mountain bike. She reminded me of Carol Klein, the TV gardener, but was fifteen or twenty years younger,

She was bouncy, chatty, full of energy and, just for a moment, made me wish I was single; but in my saddlebag was something silky from Sue's top drawer to remind me where my loyalties lay. She asked if she was the first nutter I'd met on my travels. We chatted and laughed for ten minutes or so and then she gave me instructions putting me back on route.

From there it was pretty well all downhill into Portreath, where I found my way straight to the Fountain Springs Hotel. I was greeted by the landlord, who was a lovely guy. He couldn't have been more helpful and the room, while compact, had everything and everything worked.

I'd forgotten what a disaster the newer part of Portreath is: someone in the 1960s let loose the developers in a huge way. The area around the harbour is one big housing estate of over 100 townhouses. The town has an industrial past so it may be that they cleared an area of derelict industrial land and built on it.

The beach, on the other hand, is wonderful and is a favourite place for locals to exercise their dogs. I spent a couple of hours sitting there, watching the goings on, while the sun set, leaving a wondrous afterglow.

Back at the hotel I watched England beat Russia 3 – 0 at Wembley in the European Cup qualifiers whilst writing up the day's events.

Day mileage: 46.6   Total: 512   (Max: 42.7 m.p.h.)

A typical scene on the North Cornwall coast above Portreath.

Sunset over Portreath Beach.

Thursday, 13th September 2007

A Short Day's Ride.

Portreath blessed me with a whole two hundred yards of flat road before the inevitable climb out. Half way up the hill I stopped to take a photograph of the town – well, that was my excuse...

At this point, I had completed 500 miles from Lowestoft but was unaware of this because, as I was to discover later, I'd forgotten to attach my handlebar computer before starting off. I was two miles down the road before I realised that the computer was still in the handlebar bag and recording nothing.

The situation was soon rectified but it would mean another little adjustment to the figures at the end of the day, to try and keep tabs on my true mileage.

Only a few miles along the road, but two hours after breakfast, I was seduced by the sign outside the Hell's Mouth Café, which promised "Delicious Coffee". I went inside and asked the delicious young lady for a cup and it *was* delicious.

Sitting in the sunshine, I noticed that people on the cliff edge across the road were busily taking photographs so, when I'd finished my coffee, I wandered over with my camera to see what was catching their attention. I found that they were looking at some spectacular cliff scenery in perfect morning light. The views were the sort that attract artists and make me wish I was one but I had to make do with my own couple of photographs.

Another cyclist was enjoying the view and we chatted for a while. A lovely native Cornishman, about my age, he told me that this was his regular run on his Saracen mountain bike. He said that if he ever found a problem with the bike he brought it out to this cliff-top, turned it upside down and worked on it there. "Is there a better workshop anywhere?" he asked.

Whilst breezing along the almost level road across the cliff-top, I thought back to mornings near Waddesdon and Drayton where I saw so many grim faced commuters, racing to the office. "It's good, being sixty two and retired" I thought.

The centre of old Portreath, with the remains of the former mineral railway.

Hell's Mouth.

All too soon, I reached Hayle, a town with nothing special to make me want to stop. On the road out of town, I found some confusion over which side-road I needed to take to follow my intended route.

With a little intuition and a lot of luck, I muddled through to St Erth, not entirely via the pink line on the map but never far from it, and there I promptly strayed again! However, I was soon back on track and heading down the back road towards Marazion with the main road and its traffic, plus the railway line to Penzance away to my right.

A gently undulating ride brought me out above Marazion and soon I was looking out over the bay at a hazy St Michael's Mount with the tide receding to reveal the causeway that leads out to it.

As I was getting into the popular end of Cornwall, I had pre-booked a bed in the Mount View Hotel two days earlier. I spent ten minutes hunting around Marazion for the hotel before discovering that it is actually a mile along the coast at Longrock.

Even so, I was settled into my room by twelve thirty and eating lunch in the bar before one o'clock. This had turned out to be a short day as a result of yesterday's fairly long one.

It was well within my grasp to thrash on to Land's End, finish in a blaze of glory and return to the hotel for the night. In retrospect, that's exactly what I should have done. Instead I made my way along the water's edge to pay my first ever visit to Saint Michael's Mount.

It seemed a little unworldly to be strolling along the beach, with time on my hands, instead of pressing on and clocking up the miles, as I had become accustomed to do.

Even more unworldly was the sight of a cluster of ramshackle wooden buildings, between the beach and the railway, decorated with four mermaids, painted on plywood cut-outs and adorned with old fishing nets.

Saint Michael's mount.

A beautiful TR6. (The car next door is locked up with a window wide open!)

A fisherman's harem – four sirens of the sea.

The view along Mounts Bay from Longrock to Marazion.

The causeway was high and dry, as was the beach to either side of it, and I joined a steady stream of other sightseers wandering over to the entrance to the island through a beautiful, late-summer afternoon.

Strolling round the water's edge on the way to the Mount.

Having paid my £6.50 to the National Trust, I made the hot, hard slog up through the gardens to the castle. Once there, however, the cooling breeze and the lovely views made it all worthwhile.

The Castle. The lady in the pink top reminded me of Sue.

The harbour and the causeway leading back to Marazion.

From the battlements, I watched the incoming tide encroach on and then envelop the causeway back to the mainland. A few hardy souls waded through while those of a more cautious disposition turned back and made for the harbour to catch the first boat.

Decision time on the causeway.

From 400BC to 400 AD the island was an important port for the export of tin and copper to the Europe. In 1075, following the Norman conquest, St Michael's Mount was granted to the French Mont St Michel, presumably acquiring its name at that time.

It remained in their possession until 1414 when it was appropriated as an alien priory and then granted to Syon Abbey in 1424 by Henry VI.

In 1659 Colonel St Aubyn purchased the Mount and his family have held it to the present day, although ownership was taken over by the National Trust in 1954 with the Aubyn family holding a 999 year lease.

In 1846 Queen Victoria and Prince Albert made an impromptu visit whilst cruising in the Britannia. In the absence of the family, the royal guests were entertained by the housekeeper. That must have caused a stir when the family returned home and found out whom they had missed!

There was a further royal visitor in 1902 when Edward VII came to call. As a result of a tipsy fisherman spitting at the King's feet, Lord St Levan closed down the St Aubyn Arms pub. There doesn't seem to be a record of the fate of the fisherman.

When I'd finished exploring and learning about the history of the Mount, I treated myself to a proper Cornish ice-cream and then went down to the harbour, where I hopped on a boat to cross from this temporary island back to the mainland.

Since I was nearing the end of the ride, I seized the opportunity to do a spot of gift shopping in Marazion before taking a slow, barefoot stroll along the beach back to Longrock, the Mount View Hotel, dinner and bed.

Day mileage: 18.9   Total: 530

Friday, 14th September 2007

Land's End = Journey's End.

Another sunny morning greeted me on my Day of Destiny and for a change I had a completely flat first couple of miles cycling into Penzance. There is a smooth trail along the back of the beach, separated from the railway by a chain-link fence and I breezed along into the town, meeting one or two other cyclists and a few joggers.

The way into Penzance, approaching the gaping front of the railway terminus.

The cycle trail was a real boon, by-passing the A30 with all of its roundabouts and heavy traffic. It carried me right through to the lower part of Penzance, from where I could fiddle my way through the side streets, up into the town centre.

I paused to photograph some interesting old buildings as I went. They included Captain Cutter's House, which apparently had been a tobacconist's since the eighteenth century, and the Admiral Benbow Inn where there seemed to be some sort of drama in progress...

Smoking was good for you in 1789.

"Where's that feckless, no-good villain gone now?"

In Market Jew Street I bought twenty five postcards of Land's End on the (wrong) assumption that they would be cheaper there than at Land's End itself. Having bought stamps for the postcards, I dropped back down to the sea-front and trundled along to Newlyn.

Flags outside the Queen's Hotel, on the sea-front.

I enjoyed a nice cup of coffee in the sunshine outside a pretty little café. Whilst relaxing, I saw two ladies in a panic when they realised that they'd lost an old gent who must have had Alzheimer's disease. While they'd fussed over coffee and what cakes to have, he had simply wandered off to have a look around.

They soon found him and brought him back, scolding him gently. I think everyone knew it was their lapse in not keeping an eye on him. Mind you, I don't envy anyone having the responsibility of caring for a victim of that horrible disease.

Back on the bike, I rode past a fish processing plant – the second one on this journey and older than the Lowestoft one – up onto the A30 and turned west for the last few miles to Land's End. I was prepared to put up with the moderate traffic on this A-road to avoid the steep gradients on the back roads via Mousehole.

The old milepost at Crows an Wra told me exactly what the position was.

Passing Crows an Wra, I made a note of the entrance to my B&B stop at Treave, already booked for that night, which was set back from the road down a drive. I had phoned ahead three days previously and when I spoke to the landlady, Jill, she had said in her broad Cornish accent "We're clean but we're not posh" and laughed. I knew at once that I was going to like her.

With such a short distance to cover I reached Sennen village just after midday and had parked myself in the Famous First and Last Inn by ten past. For no particular reason I had decided to arrive at the end of my journey at 2.18 – exactly two weeks after starting out. This left me two hours to idle away at the pub.

I simply had to have a pint of Skinners' First and Last Ale (in a Tribute glass) in the fading sunshine out in the pub garden. I followed up with a superb ploughman's lunch of locally smoked mackerel – surely, therefore, a fisherman's lunch – plus a second pint to celebrate my impending achievement.

So there I was, within sight of my destination, one mile to go and I sat and looked at it for two hours on a whim. I suppose it was my tidy mind but if I'd had any sense at all, I would have cracked on to the end and come back to the pub afterwards.

With fifteen minutes to go, impatience got the better of me and I started off down the road. I stopped several times to take photographs and still had to dawdle to avoid arriving early. The sky had clouded over completely so putting on my long-sleeved jersey took up another couple of minutes. This was getting very silly.

The Land's End "theme park".

Entering the Land's End complex, I sidestepped all the commercialised noise and glitz to go straight down to the actual, geographical point. After 541 safe miles, I almost fell off the bike whilst getting out the camera (I was still going along at the time!) and setting it to video to record my arrival at journey's end.

With the camera running, I freewheeled down the track to the low wall guarding the cliffs. The camera recorded the immortal words "That's it – there's nowhere else to go". At 2.18, I was there.

After a totally dry fortnight, two minutes after I arrived it began to drizzle – a fitting commentary on the less than dramatic end to the epic. I should have crashed on to the end the previous day and finished with a sense of achievement. But I had done it.

Not really knackered – just ducking my head to show the sign.

After having my photo taken I went up to the "theme park" and paid an exorbitant amount for a cup of tea and then rode back up the A30 to Treave, to meet landlady Jill and her husband Terry. The welcome was as warm as I had expected and I soon settled in.

Having showered and changed, I rode down to Sennen Post Office & Stores and back to get some grub, since it wasn't available at Treave. It was strange to feel the bike so light and responsive without the saddlebag on the back.

Day mileage: 22.9   Total: 553

A card which I received from friends.

Saturday, 15th September 2007

Exploring the Far West.

I woke to a beautiful, post-cold front day with limitless visibility and wall to wall blue sky. My immediate thought was that it was a perfect day for aviation so, after breakfast, I cycled over to Land's End Airport.

However, their scenic flights pilot wasn't there. They said I could hang on in the hope of sneaking a flight in the instructor's aircraft between lessons but nothing was certain. Having a) hung around a lot of airfields in my time and b) done the Land's End scenic flight before – 26½ years before – I decided to abandon the idea and move on.

Enjoying the luxury of riding *sans* saddlebag, I breezed down to Sennen Cove, where I wrote and posted my twenty five postcards announcing my success. I took a leisurely wander around the village, reviving memories of my last stay there, back in 1977 when I spent a week based at the Old Success Inn. (It would have been quite appropriate to stay there now but they were fully booked). Thirty years later the main change was the increase in the number of cars.

Looking out on the Atlantic over Sennen Cove.

I bought a gift for Sue and then sat with a cup of coffee and watched the surfers for a while. Even without the saddlebag, the hill out of the village was too fiendishly steep for me and I walked the second half up to the cliff top. I lay on the grass and enjoyed a different perspective on the surfers, as well as the panoramic views.

For lunch I trolleyed along to the Famous First and Last Inn, where the landlady, Daphne, greeted me like an old friend after the previous day's visit. Once again I sat in the sunshine and wrapped myself around a pint of First and Last Ale and a smoked mackerel ploughman's – *fisherman's* - lunch.

I witnessed a heart-warming sight when an aged gentleman turned up, only to discover that he had brought no money with him. Daphne sat him down, brought out a pint and then delivered a sausage sandwich with all the trimmings. He sang her praises to me as he left after his meal. As he said, she is a good woman.

Jill, the landlady at my B&B, had told me about a little cove called Penberth and I decided to give it a go. I found it easily and was delighted to discover a completely un-commercialised and unspoilt little hamlet hidden away down a lane. It offers tourists no facilities whatever apart from one bench seat and lots of footpaths.

At the top of the slipway was a modern, electric winch for pulling up boats from the water's edge and behind that was a restored and preserved wooden winch which must have been the original means of doing the same job. It was in beautiful condition – obviously the result of a great deal of effort on somebody's part.

I wandered around rather self-consciously, as the locals outnumbered us Emmets by about three to one. Then I hopped back on the bike to ford the small stream which flows through the village.

Parking the bike on the other side I looked around for a few minutes and then set off up a stepped path through the bracken. The main reason for this was that my lunchtime pint was outstaying its welcome. Once that problem was solved I carried on up as the views – firstly of the village and then of the surrounding cliffs – just got better and better.

Penberth, with a local fisherman's family waiting on the slipway for his return.

The seaward end of Penberth Cove.

I arrived on the cliff top, overlooking Logan Rock and along to Porthcurno to the west and all the way to Porthleven and Loe Bar, across Mounts Bay to the east. I found a comfortable spot and settled on the cliff top for an hour (or two – I really have no idea).

Fishing boats and sailing boats meandered around on a millpond sea while ships crept along the horizon. Helicopters and planes to-ed and fro-ed between the Scillies and the mainland and the Cessna from Land's End airport made occasional sorties. Had things worked out better in the morning, I would have been up there looking down...

I developed a fascination for one little fishing boat and took several pictures of it as it worked its way past me, heading east. Then it was time to go and as I came over the hill above Penbarth, there was the same little fishing boat, just approaching the slipway.

I was witness to a scene the basics of which have remained unchanged over thousands of years. The fisherman's wife, a well-rounded lady who laughed a lot, had pulled out the winch cable to the water's edge, ready for his arrival and the boat was soon drawn up to the top of the slipway where there was a family gathering around it.

The days catch of mackerel and sea bass was unloaded in leisurely fashion, inspected by the gathered family and friends, then gutted over the stream so that the innards were recycled efficiently back to the sea for the gulls.

First glimpse.

The fisherman is met with the winch cable by his wife.

The boat being winched up the slipway.

Gutting and cleaning the day's catch over the stream.

Afternoon tea called, so I collected the bike and pottered off up the lane back to the main road. At Trevescan I found a little café where I had a pot of tea and a piece of very nice, moist chocolate cake. I also met Oscar the dog, who wandered amiably amongst rabbits, chickens, guinea pigs and other assorted animals.

I got chatting to a couple in the café garden and told them about my sponsored ride. When I mentioned Noah's Ark Trust, they announced that they were from Malvern! By the time they left we had compared notes on most of the pubs around Malvern and Ledbury. It truly is a small world.

I headed on down to Land's End and set up camp on the most westerly bench seat in England. The sky was cloudless again by now and I watched the sea; I watched the birds; I watched the boats and I watched the planes. I even watched the other watchers.

A glimpse of a seal's head in the turbulent water around the rocks sent me scurrying to get my binoculars from the bike. I watched some more, waited and, sure enough, after a few minutes he (or she) reappeared in the same patch of water, floated for a while re-oxygenating his blood and then showed a flash of shiny back as he returned to his fishing.

Deciding that there was nowhere better to spend my final evening in Cornwall, I jumped on the bike and nipped up to Sennen Stores & Post Office, a mile and a quarter up the road, to buy my evening meal. Laden with a pasty (hot), a Danish apple cake, two bottles of drink and a chocolate bar I dropped back down to Land's End to resume my vigil.

The seal had moved to the other side of the rocks and only appeared a few more times before disappearing for the night. I turned my concentration to the pasty.

Gradually the number of people dwindled as evening meals and entertainment beckoned. Eventually there were only three of us left but then the discerning – and quiet – few began to arrive. The vibe changed from noisy, ice-cream toting trippers to something peaceful and quite spiritual as the sun crept closer to the horizon.

I would have loved to stay there until dark but I was riding a fine line as I had nearly four miles to cycle to my digs at Treave with only a back light. I moved up to the hotel on the cliffs and spent a while messing about taking photos of the sunset through my polarising sunglasses to capture the colour without the glare. From there the Longships lighthouse, a mile and a half away, was directly in front of the sun and made a beautiful picture.

As so often happens, there is a powerful tug at the heartstrings when the end of a holiday approaches as if to say "Don't go – you like it here".

When I dared leave it no longer I hopped onto the bike and did a rapid four mile dash up the A30, with my tail light flashing, watching the last of the sunset over the sea to my left. Back at Treave I stashed the bike in its hideaway, down the drive from the house, and went in to chat with Jill and Terry before going up to write the diary and prepare for the journey home.

Day mileage: 34.1   Total: 587

Land's End's Farewell.

Sunday, 16th September 2007

Looking Back.

For the first time since leaving Lowestoft, I had time pressures this morning as I had to get to Penzance in time to catch the train to Cheltenham. After breakfast I packed up, made sure I'd got everything, bade farewell to Jill and Terry and hit the road.

Just on a mile up the road I realised that I *hadn't* got everything – I'd managed to leave the handlebar computer behind! I retraced my steps to Treave and knocked on the door which, fortunately, was open. No reply. I called out but no answer was forthcoming.

There was no time for courtesy – I went in and dashed up to the bedroom. The bed was already completely stripped and there was the computer, on the chest of drawers. I grabbed it, took it downstairs and put it in its mount on the handlebars. There was still no sign of my hosts and so, once again, I hit the road.

Despite the false start, I reached Penzance Station with an hour and a quarter to spare, parked the bike and went to buy some lunch for the train journey. I also bought a cheapo, metal "Kernow" flag key-ring which joined the Santiago pilgrim's shell and the Lowestoft golly on my saddlebag.

Once I'd fathomed the complexities of the Virgin Trains cycle rack and got the bike safely stashed in the guard's compartment of the train, I settled into my reserved seat and braced myself for my return to modern, high speed travel.

Spot on time, we rolled out of Penzance and accelerated along the coast. With nothing to occupy me but the blur of the West Country flying past the window, I cast my mind back over the journey.

My choice of that fortnight, because of the likelihood of dry weather, had certainly paid off. The high pressure west of Ireland, which thwarted the dreaded prevailing south-westerly wind, was an unexpected bonus. So overall the weather had been very kind to me.

The only surplus weight in my kit was from contingency insurances such as waterproof coat, lightweight body-warmer, some just-in-case medications and puncture outfit. Although essential cargo they were – happily – never needed. Everything else was used on the trip.

Apart from the one truck driver in Wiltshire, who was prepared to risk my life rather than lose momentum, everyone I met was courteous, kind and friendly. Some really were delightful and brightened my days.

I was still bemused by my experience at the Saint George Inn at Uffculme, where the breakfast was a choice between do it yourself or do without, but even there the welcome was warm and friendly. It's just that I don't like unsolved riddles.

It is an incredible tribute to British map-makers – justifiably acknowledged as the best in the world – that I could sit at home with a road atlas and plan a journey of more than 500 miles across the country on small roads, some of which had grass growing down the middle. It struck me more than once how bizarre it was to be cycling down one of these small, winding lanes and yet be on the way across the country.

The only really bad road that I experienced was one which should have been totally reliable since it was a "B" road, not a lane, and that was down to Essex County Council and not the map-makers.

I had never really thought before that a cyclist is always going to cover more than a mile for every mile of road, simply because one has to weave, however gently, to balance as well as avoiding dead creatures, drains, rocks and holes.

I regularly had to drag my mind back from planning ahead or doing other "housework" to do with the ride, to concentrate on the moment and enjoy where I was and what I was doing. On the other hand, the advantage of a disorganised mind like mine is that not much of interest escaped un-noticed, be it wildlife or a distant view.

Regrets – I had a few but, then again, too few to mention. Coming across Suffolk on the second day I saw a wheelie bin fitted with Mickey Mouse ears and nose. I smiled and rode by. If only I'd known how many amusing and original wheelie bins I was to pass, I would have photographed them as a running theme through the journal. I can recall faces, flowers, street scenes, trees and exotically painted house names. By the time I realised, it was too late.

I wish I'd taken more photos of people that I met and also made a note of their names. I'd love to know how the two girls got on, on their journey to John O'Groats and that they got there safely. And it would have been good to be able to put their names on the photo.

It was late afternoon when the train reached Cheltenham Spa – still spot on time – and I changed into my shorts in the station toilet before climbing onto the bike for the final leg.

I found my way out of Cheltenham and across the M5 without any bother and once I turned north towards Tewkesbury, I had a brisk wind on my back which, with my hard-earned fitness, saw me fly up the road and through the town. I crossed the Avon and then the Severn, after which the wind was on my front quarter, and my pace reduced considerably.

I still made good time to Wellington Heath, partly because the Duke of York at Birtsmorton, where I had promised myself a pint, was closed. Even so, the light was beginning to fade by the time I parked up my bike and removed the saddle bag for the last time, twenty four miles from Cheltenham Spa station.

Needless to say, I received a hero's welcome from Sue and the two black kittens she had acquired while I was away.

The sponsored distance, from Lowestoft to Land's End, was 541 miles. As accurately as I can tell, bearing in mind the various times when I started riding without the handlebar computer connected, the total distance, home to home, was 622 miles.

The total Sponsorship raised was £714.40 and could have been more if I'd started seeking sponsors earlier and attracted more publicity.

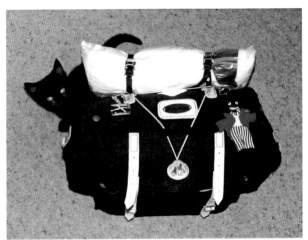

My saddlebag being examined by Guinness, one of the two new kittens.

The map on our kitchen wall on which Sue and Andy plotted my progress.

This was the first time since 1965 that I had undertaken a fortnight's cycle tour and the joy of this one made me a) regret the ones that had got away in the intervening years and b) determined to do something similar next year. Consequently as I type this, plans are well advanced for the next trip – from Lowestoft to Ardnamurchan Lighthouse, on the west coast of Scotland, the most westerly point on the British mainland, which will be around a hundred miles further than this ride. I look forward to it.